The Dimensions of Diplomacy

Books on Foreign Affairs from
The Johns Hopkins University
School of Advanced International Studies

THE ALLIANCE FOR PROGRESS: PROBLEMS AND PERSPECTIVES
John C. Dreier, ed.

EUROPEAN INTEGRATION
C. Grove Haines, ed.

ISLAMIC JURISPRUDENCE: Shāfi'ī's *Risāla*
Majid Khadduri

WAR AND PEACE IN THE LAW OF ISLAM
Majid Khadduri

NATIONALISM AND PROGRESS IN FREE ASIA
Philip W. Thayer, ed.

THE UNITED STATES AND THE UNITED NATIONS
Francis O. Wilcox and H. Field Haviland, Jr.

ALLIANCE POLICY IN THE COLD WAR
Arnold Wolfers, ed.

CHANGING EAST-WEST RELATIONS AND THE UNITY OF THE WEST
Arnold Wolfers, ed.

DISCORD AND COLLAROBATION: ESSAYS ON INTERNATIONAL POLITICS
Arnold Wolfers

THE DIMENSIONS OF DIPLOMACY
E. A. J. Johnson, ed.

THE DIMENSIONS
OF DIPLOMACY

BY
McGeorge Bundy
Henry A. Kissinger
W. W. Rostow
James R. Killian, Jr.
Adolf A. Berle
Livingston Merchant

E. A. J. Johnson, Editor

THE JOHNS HOPKINS PRESS   BALTIMORE   1964

Foreword

In 1943, under the leadership of Christian A. Herter, the School of Advanced International Studies was established in order to provide, in the nation's capital, a graduate institution for the training of young people in the increasingly important field of world affairs. Seven years later the School became an integral part of the The Johns Hopkins University. In the summer of 1963 SAIS moved into its new building at 1740 Massachusetts Avenue in Washington, D.C. This volume of lectures—delivered during the academic year 1963-64—consequently marks not only the twentieth anniversary of the founding of SAIS but also the formal dedication of our new quarters.

Once again I would like to express my profound gratitude to the six foundations (Ford, Rockefeller, Avalon, Kellogg, Old Dominion, and the Carnegie Corporation) which helped to underwrite the ten-year development program of the School in 1960 and thus made possible the construction of our handsome physical plant. My warm thanks also go to the members of the School's Advisory Council—and especially to President Milton S. Eisenhower, and Paul A. Nitze—who worked so diligently to bring the development plans to fruition. Along the way countless other friends of the School helped to convert a dream into reality. To all of them we at the School of Advanced International Studies are deeply grateful.

Francis O. Wilcox, Dean
School of Advanced International Studies
The Johns Hopkins University

In Appreciation

The Johns Hopkins School of Advanced International Studies wishes to express its special appreciation to Mr. Jacob M. Kaplan, President of the J. M. Kaplan Fund, Inc., whose interest in world affairs has enabled several students to pursue their graduate work at the School and whose generous assistance in 1963-64 made possible the dedicatory lecture series now collected in this volume.

Contents

Preface

ALTHOUGH diplomacy might be described as a complex and delicate instrument that measures the forces working at the epicenters of international relations, unlike the physicist's seismographs—which can only record disturbances—the subtle machinery of diplomacy can be used to arrest, meliorate, or reduce the discord, misunderstandings, and disagreements which precipitate international crises. Diplomacy performs this eminently useful function by patient, ceaseless, and, most often, undramatic negotiations; by alert observation; and by adherence to a pattern of useful social activity that widens the knowledge and cultural experience of foreign service officers.

On these diplomatic interchanges of ideas and on the resulting political, economic, and military interactions, the peace, progress, safety, and well-being of millions of people very greatly depend; and the more interdependent the parts of the world community become, the greater the role that diplomacy must play! For this reason a central problem of this moment of world history, when the interpenetration of events, ideas, and policies is greater than ever before, is to ascertain whether the quality of diplomacy is adequate for its tasks and whether the forms of diplomacy are properly structured. For only if diplomacy can insure really satisfactory international communication will the world community be spared the choice, not as formerly, between war and peace, but between world chaos and a tolerable world order. This is why it is so extremely important, indeed urgently important, to assess the dimensions and the capabilities of modern diplomacy.

The chapters of this book are directed to this task. Prepared as lectures arranged to commemorate the dedication of new physical facilities and the inauguration of new educational and research programs at the School of Advanced International Studies of The Johns Hopkins University, the essays of the six authors are concerned with an equal number of facets of an ever-emergent diplomacy. Admittedly, these are but a few aspects of the complex and many-sided diplomatic art, but surely scholarship, strategy, planning, science, and economics are among the more important essentials that contribute to the "techniques," to the style, and, above all, to the efficacy of diplomatic activity.

My colleagues and I are most grateful to the distinguished contributors to this joint effort, particularly since each of them is faced with such insistent duties in the public interest. That they were willing to find time to prepare these lectures is surely an indication of their conviction that the university is still the true sanctuary for all who believe in the enriching influence of active minds, and in the puissant utility of learning for such practical tasks as designing new bridges of human understanding.

E. A. J. JOHNSON

The Dimensions of Diplomacy

I

The Battlefields of Power and the Searchlights of the Academy

McGeorge Bundy

i

So VAST indeed is the set of connections which now bind the world of power and the world of learning that it is a matter of the greatest difficulty to isolate particular parts of the connection for close analysis. Moreover, the designers of this set of essays have complicated my own task by assigning the more visible elements of the problem to later speakers, who are going to discuss the scientific problems of the new diplomacy and its strategic and economic problems. The importance of these topics is enormous; it is right that they should have attention, and my own comments can best begin with a brief look at these relatively well-defined connections.

I believe that the progress of science has made a genuine revolution in the realities of human affairs. The advance in our control over nature, and still more the pace of advance, have created a fully new situation with sweeping requirements for new thought and action. This is most obvious in the field of strategic weapons, but other powerful connections between science and politics are foreshadowed in such fields as population, the desalting of sea water, and the understanding of weather. In such areas, self-evidently, there is a necessary and constantly expanding process of connection between the university and the government.

In the field of economic thought and action, the interlocking is at least as clear and perhaps a little more familiar. Without an understanding of economists—and of their importance in public affairs—there can be no true understanding of the political history of the nations of the West in the last thirty years. There may be an argument about the degree of influence of the great economists of earlier times—from Adam Smith on down—but neither the friends nor the enemies of John Maynard Keynes have doubted his practical importance. The close and growing connection between the economists of the academy and the process of government is both cause and consequence of this reality. It is at least possible that this connection, by its very strength and self-confidence, may now be threatened by some of the rigidities of a satisfied orthodoxy. But if reform is needed, it is unlikely to come from divorce.

A third special area of powerful professional connection between the higher learning and government is the field of area studies. It is a curious fact of academic history that the first great center of area studies in the United States was not located in any university, but in Washington, during the Second World War, in the Office of Strategic Services. In very large measure the area study programs developed in American universities in the years after the war were manned, directed, or stimulated by graduates of the OSS—a remarkable institution, half cops-and-robbers and half faculty meeting. It is still true today, and I hope it always will be, that there is a high measure of interpenetration between universities with area programs and the information-gathering agencies of the government of the United States.

Area studies have a special meaning for the new diplomacy, going well beyond their practical importance for men who have to make decisions affecting little-known parts of the world. Area studies constitute the first explicit recognition, in the main-stream of American intellectual history, of the simple proposition that people are different. At the time of Woodrow Wilson, it was the articulate major premise of our democracy, and the inarticulate major premise of our new diplomacy, that people are not deeply different from one another. It followed that one could and should think of making the world safe for democracy by ways and means drawn directly from the American political tradition.[1]

Now we assume the opposite. We expect to find deep differences among the peoples of the world. We do not believe that the Soviet mind works like ours or that African society will operate as ours does. This assumption and expectation of variety affects our behavior and will affect it more as the continued growth of experience and the continued expansion of study enlarge the impact of this new

---

[1] This simple error can be demonstrated, I believe, in the intellectual history of Woodrow Wilson—and it is part of the tragic irony of Wilson's history that this assessment did not even correctly reflect the American reality itself.

perception upon some of our more traditional processes of analysis and action.

Still another special subject of great interest to the contemporary academic scholar is the general area of contemporary issues in the foreign policy of the United States itself. Where these problems are centrally political, they will not usually fall within any one of the fields I have already mentioned. There are some in government who believe that at the active edge of present policy-making, the role of the universities should be small, and their opinions are shared by some in the universities who are made uncomfortable by colleagues whose scholarship is not safely specialized or dated. But for myself, I think it right that universities should be deeply engaged in these matters—that there should be people who are for or against the proposal for a Multilateral Force; for or against a general policy of easing tensions with the Soviet Union; for or against a given framework for a foreign aid program; for or against the strengthening of the United Nations, not merely as an instrument of policy but in some measure as an object of policy too. But it makes little difference, practically, whether one approves or disapproves of this interest and activity. It is a fact that professors and students will concern themselves with these things and that therefore this kind of connection, too, will bind the university to the problems of the new diplomacy.

Sweeping as this summary of subjects has been, it is not in fact what I wish to discuss. I have listed them and commented on them mainly to set them up as a background to other questions which are less easy to discuss but perhaps even more important. Science and economics, the new societies and the current issues, are all indispensable parts of the new diplomacy, but they do not go to its heart.

ii

The heart of the matter here, as in all politics, is to be found in power and purpose, and the question for this essay is the question of the proper role of the academy for our time on these great issues. A question so large can have only fragments of an answer. I offer five such fragments. The validity of each seems to me real, and I shall offer argument that they can be connected sensibly each to the other. How much of the whole they may represent is another matter about which I make no claim.

Two of my fragments are philosophic. If you press the question of purpose in any area of politics, you are forced back to philosophy. This is true not only of the central issue of power but of the specific topics which we have just summarized. A technical, an economic, or a strategic problem will in the end become a problem of purpose. A recommended policy must have an object, and the object must be justified by standards of value or conviction. Behind all technical counsel there will be intent.

It is the very beginning of academic wisdom to recognize that a university by its very nature must be concerned with these matters. In that sense, philosophy must remain in the center of the mission of the academy. If it has not philosophy, in this sense, the university necessarily becomes a kind of denial that there is meaning or purpose in society itself.

For reasons which deserve respect, many outstanding members of the American academy are suspicious of any insistence upon the teaching of values. The fear of indoctrination and cant is justified, and the most self-consciously righteous of our institutions are often the least enlightened. Yet there is no escape from the problem of purpose, and if it be excluded from departments of philosophy, it will re-enter in a hundred other places. The question of purpose is posed by the very presence of the young, and answers to the question are implicit in every concrete action of the academy. The teaching of purpose is literally inescapable. The problem is only one of doing it well, because it gets done in one way or other—whether or not that is the intent of the institution, and whether or not the men who are doing it know what they are doing.

My own conviction is that it helps to recognize this reality. I grant that an argument can be made against such recognition, but I doubt if it can be pressed with good grace from the academy itself. Institutions built on a fundamental commitment to the truth must find it awkward to assert that it helps to ignore the most obvious reality of their activity.

The university cannot help itself then; it teaches purpose whether it will or not. And for our present topic two kinds of purpose deserve attention: the purpose of the citizen and the purpose of the state. Each of these topics, of course, is confronted by departments of government and departments of philosophy. But I am not here to talk about standard courses in civics or even in political philosophy, important as such studies are. Indeed, my suggestion is that these questions are much wider than is suggested by the arbitrary barriers of incomplete disciplines which have divided the academic catalogues and subdivided the academic faculties. The examination of the purpose of an American citizen is not something which one would necessarily find in a department of philosophy, and never in a department of philosophy alone.

What is needed, I suggest, is a wider and more conscious process of examination—of what it is that we ourselves are for and what in consequence may be the purpose of our national power. There has been in this generation, throughout our society, too ready an assumption that these questions do not need examination. We have assumed that the role of the citizen is clear and the legitimate purpose of the nation well known. These assumptions are open to doubt, and when doubts are not explored in departments of philosophy or politics, they will creep in again, through other departments. Not merely in the new social sciences, not merely in the academy as a whole, but in the assumptions and behavior of our whole people there is today a question as to the clarity and coherence both of our purposes as citizens and the complementary purpose of our government. History has outrun thought, and our practice is no longer clearly based on our convictions.

I am far from asserting that we face a breakdown of the national will or that our current political life has been falsified. The revolution in our national position has been so swift and sweeping that it is no more than natural that the doctrines of political philosophy have been outrun. Judged against what might reasonably have been expected a generation ago, the performance of our people and even of our government in this new age has been remarkable.

Measured against the record of others, moreover, the breakdown in the relation between what we do and what we
believe seems less severe in the United States than in any
other major nation. Yet such relative success gives no final
comfort. No society can survive indefinitely if there is
serious separation between what it believes and what it
does, and no academy can avoid the challenge to attack
that separation without a betrayal of its own central
meaning.

I intend here no abdication of the functions of the government itself. In the short run, and sometimes for the
longer range as well, the definition of purpose and the
effective connection between that purpose and performance
are the responsibility of those who hold and use power, and
in particular of the President of the United States. The
Presidents of the last three years have recognized and accepted this responsibility and would smile at my suggestion that this task be referred back to the professors.

But in the larger sense the challenge to the academy remains. The philosophy of the American, and the philosophy
of America, are ripe for redefinition.

iii

While we wait for a renewed philosophy, there is another
set of questions which are deeply and immediately urgent
for people who are themselves in government. These are
questions not about the purpose of politics but about its
ways and means. And here I believe there are great opportunities for a much wider and stronger connection between

universities and governments than we yet have. Certainly there is now no shortage of academic inquiry into the nature of politics. There is enough, and perhaps too much, analysis aimed at scholarly rigor and scientific validity. There is enough and perhaps too much system-building in which models of this or that political process are constructed. There is enough, and perhaps too much, detailed historical recording of political phenomena. What there is not enough of yet, and what I come to praise, is the kind of academic work which proceeds from the same center of concern as that of the man who is himself committed to an active part in government. That center of concern is the taking and use of power itself.

For this kind of work I find no better word than history. I do not here mean departments of history any more than earlier I meant departments of philosophy. I am talking about history generically, as an account of events, of people concerned with events, and of the way in which the people and the events interact, around the central theme of political power. People who are locked in the process of government grope for enlightenment from history as a record of the performance of individuals or groups of individuals connected to particular political events. The history which keeps its focus on the pursuit and use of political power is the history to which politicians and diplomats, old and new, most naturally turn when they seek enlightenment, or even entertainment. This is the type of activity, in universities, which can most immediately contribute to the wider education and re-education of political men.

I suggest three particular kinds of history which have this relevance. The first is personal history, which takes the form either of autobiography or of biography. The beginning of the process of politics is the man. It is only the beginning, but it is where we have to start.

Autobiography and biography have contrasting advantages and disadvantages. Political autobiography has the enormous advantage that the author was in the process; he was there, and his reader can become engaged directly with him. The autobiographer may or may not have some capacity for detachment. He may or may not have a sense of events wider than his own field of action. But at least he begins with a personal acquaintance with the process, and even unintentionally he will almost always convey something about the reality of that process. So the autobiography of the political man is one of the indispensable instruments for the understanding of politics.

Yet the biographer too has great advantages. He is not so limited in vision. Although he may become the apologist of his subject, he is at least not the captive of his subject's vanity, and vanity is only too frequent in political circles, especially among those who take time to write books about themselves. Yet if the biographer has the advantage of a certain detachment, he runs the risk of not feeling the flame of politics as it really is. He runs the risk of the critic who does not fully understand the pleasure or the pain, the temptation or the triumph, of the player.

Here we come to a point which has struck me with great force, as an amateur come late to the world of active political life. Among serious, full-time professional political men one finds an enormous sense of comradeship which derives from their understanding of the fact that they are in an embattled profession. Your political man, whether in a democracy or a dictatorship, commits himself to the pursuit of power. For those who would succeed greatly, this pursuit is passionate and preemptive. It requires an enormous commitment of ambition, and whether power and position are conferred by public approval or by higher authority, your political leader has placed the meaning of his life at the disposal of others than himself. He has placed himself at the mercy of forces beyond his full control, and his political life is staked at intervals, just as a soldier's life is staked upon a battle. To be committed to the pursuit of power, even in the most civilized of societies, is to take chances that others do not take. Politicians in democratic societies are frequently the objects of a generalized public contempt. When such contempt is expressed by men who should know better, it becomes merely one more obstacle to understanding and to mutual respect. A short way of describing one purpose of this essay is to say that there is every reason for the American university to find ways and means of responding to the reality of American political life as it is seen by those who live it.

A second form of history which is instructive and attractive to men engaged immediately in government is what we call "case history." While personal history is indispensable, it suffers the great disadvantage that even in the most generous of hands it is individual in focus. While man may be the beginning of the process of politics, he is not the process itself. The intertwining of persons, purposes, and institutions is different from the life of the individual in all kinds of ways. These differences are illuminated by case history, which is a new phrase for an old process. It is a good phrase, and great credit must go to those who initiated modern case history, whether in law or in business or in public administration. The object of such history is to take a set of events with some definable beginning and ending and to find out what really happened—to assess the motivations, the behavior, and the effectiveness of the individual's concern and to make a kind of reaction, or perhaps a dramatization, of this set of events so that the student can learn from a sample of the process of politics.

Case history is as old as the Greeks, but today there is special value in case histories of very recent events, simply because of the degree to which circumstances have been changed by the special forces of science and technology. For example, it is hard to take an issue like the organization of the nuclear defense of Europe and find relevant parallel problems anywhere but in contemporary studies. I believe there is every reason for encouraging the closest possible interpenetration of students and of performers so that this kind of assessment can be a part of the regular business of contemporary life.

Partly because of its origins in public administration and partly because of the difficulties of analysis and reconstruction, case history can suffer from the weakness of detachment. Too often it is the premise of case history that it should lead to better organization of the government. Organization is an interesting, important, and difficult problem, but it is not a problem which touches the heart of the process of politics. A part of the remedy here is that case histories should be informed by a deeper sense of the realities of power and its use, but in the end I think we must seek a wider framework. If the history of the indi-

vidual is not quite at the center, and if the case history remains an incomplete method, what else is there?

My third class of history, to which I myself would give
first prize, is as hard to name as it is important. The best
that I have been able to do is to borrow a phrase from
Professor John Finley and call it "disappointed history."
It is the history written by men who understand politics
because of their own initial commitment to its ambitions
and its dangers—men who have adventured in politics and
who have been forced for one reason or another to with-
draw, men who then use their feelings and concern as
observers of political events. The greatest of these his-
torians—at least the greatest that I know well enough to
talk about—is also the earliest, Thucydides. Here is how
Professor Finley describes him in a brilliant introduction to
his *History*: ". . . he watched from a distance while others
played parts on the bright and animated stage of Athenian
life. From this isolation come traits suggestive of the
later exile, Dante, and the cast-off politician, Machiavelli:
detachment from, yet obsession with, politics, the observer's
capacity to categorize and distill, joined with the suppressed
passion bred of disappointment."[2]

Over and over again Thucydides goes to the center of
what really moved people. Right at the beginning of his
history he asks what the Peloponnesian War was about:
"To the question why they broke the treaty, I answer by
placing first an account of their grounds of complaint and
points of difference, that no one may ever have to ask the

---

[2] John H. Finley (ed.), *The Complete Writings of Thucydides* (New York:
The Modern Library), p. viii.

immediate cause which plunged the Hellenes into a war of such magnitude. The real cause I consider to be the one which was formally most kept out of sight. The growth of the power of Athens, and the alarm which this inspired in Lacedaemon, made war inevitable. Still it is well to give the grounds alleged by either side, which led to the dissolution of the treaty and the breaking out of the war."[3]

That alleged reasons and real reasons are not always the same is a cliché of historical writing, but this passage combines awareness of the two kinds of reality with respect for both of them; this is unusual, I think, except among men like Thucydides who have had a direct exposure to politics by their own choice and commitment.

Whether he is discussing the difficulties natural to a coalition, in the famous passage forcefully repeated by President Kennedy at Frankfurt in 1963, or laying bare in a dozen different speeches the ways in which democratic politics interact with the conduct of war, Thucydides goes always to the political heart of the matter. He holds his light on the great linked realities of political life: the pursuit of power and its active use. To Thucydides the field of political action has the reality the battlefield has for a retired soldier: his *History* is inconceivable except as the product of deep political experience.

Dangerous as it may be to draw general conclusions from single cases, I venture the suggestion that the *History* of Thucydides presents us with the question whether we have ways and means of encouraging this kind of work by disappointed politicians in our own society. I do not say that there will be many like Thucydides or that you can

---

[3] *Ibid.*, p. 15.

create such men merely by firing politicians; disappointment does not always breed detachment and passion does not guarantee perceptiveness. Still I suggest that in the life of our universities there is much room for men writing the kind of history which is possible only when there is a deep engagement of sympathy to the battlefield of politics and to the way the men on that battlefield conceive of their war. I think it is wrong to suppose that the university is usefully disconnected from this reality. I think rather that there is gain for both the political world and the academy from an intensified process of engagement and of choosing sides and of engaging in the battle. I do not believe that the perception and communication of reality which will properly educate the citizens of the future are possible without a strong and lively sense of what it is to be committed to the pursuit and use of political authority.

More broadly still, I believe that this element of political engagement is only a special case of a more general proposition: that the university, while nourishing inquiry at all the edges of learning, while maintaining detachment and offering sanctuary, while properly offering the moral equivalent of the exile of Thucydides, must offer these things not only to people who commit themselves finally to academic life but also to people who come and go. This is, I think, the right and necessary tendency of the best of our contemporary universities. I believe that the universities which have moved in this direction have chosen wisely, both for their own purposes and for the welfare of society. Johns Hopkins is such a university, and for me it has been a pleasure and an honor to give you even this imperfect fragment of an inaugural lecture.

II

Reflections on
Power and Diplomacy

Henry A. Kissinger

i

THE TECHNICAL characteristics of modern weapons are well known. We are aware that humanity has the power to destroy itself in a matter of hours. Any place on the earth can be reached from any other in minutes. Offensive power has far outstripped defensive power. Even a defense that is 90 per cent effective may not be able to prevent catastrophic damage.

But the conclusion to be drawn from this state of affairs is not so obvious. Some believe that if the risks have become incomparably greater, the essential priciples of strategy have stayed the same. For others war has become unthinkable, and they ask that diplomacy settle all conflicts essentially through the exercise of negotiating skill.

Each view has its difficulty. If massive quantitative changes can bring about qualitative ones, then the increase in destructiveness threatened by nuclear weapons must be considered crucial. A basic discontinuity is established when a statesman is compelled to risk tens of millions of lives instead of thousands, when his decision no longer involves the loss of a province but the survival of society itself. Even if the classical principles of strategy are not entirely outmoded, the statesman will inevitably be reluctant to put them to the test.

However, to say that the unqualified reign of diplomacy has begun is an equal oversimplification. If war has now become only the last resort of desperate men, this has not made diplomacy any easier. On the contrary, it has made it more intractable. In the past, unsuccessful negotiations never returned matters to their starting point; they called other pressures into play. But many of these pressures are no longer available, and thus diplomacy, too, has become less flexible. Where no penalty for non-compliance exists, there is no incentive to reach agreement. As statesmen have become increasingly reluctant to resort to war, they have been less eager to engage in serious negotiations. Therefore, any assessment of the impact of power on diplomacy must begin with a discussion of the characteristics of power in the nuclear age. A few definitions may be useful.

Offensive power is the ability of a political unit to impose its will on another.

Defensive power is the ability of a state to avoid coercion by another. Defensive power may be further subdivided into purely defensive policy and precautionary policy. Power has a purely defensive use when a country waits for a threat to materialize before dealing with it. It is used in a precautionary manner when policy is directed toward preventing possible and not actual challenges. The policy of the United States before World War II was purely defensive, its tendency being to allow threats to become unambiguous and then to muster every effort to overcome them. This could be afforded because the wide margin of survival guaranteed that no conceivable early reverse could menace the national interest. Britain's policy in the eighteenth and nineteenth century illustrates the precautionary mode of action. Britain acted on the diplomatic principle that Antwerp must not fall into the hands of the major powers. This was not because of any certainty that such an event would have hostile implications, but rather because Britain would no longer be strong enough to resist if the worst occurred.

Deterrent power is the ability to prevent certain threats or actions from being carried out by posing an equivalent or greater threat.

There is no inevitable symmetry between offensive and defensive power. Some states have had little of the first but much of the second. Switzerland, for example, has managed to combine inaccessibility of terrain with the ability to mobilize a considerable proportion of the national resources. States in this position have been able to prevent other countries from imposing their will. On the other hand, they have not played a very active role in international affairs.

Power has no absolute measurement; it is always relative. In the seventeenth century it would have been futile to try to compare the power of China and that of France, since they possessed no means of bringing their strength to bear on each other. This geographical separation of power remained a fact until the middle of the nineteenth century. And after that, one small continent, Europe, was physically far superior to the rest and could dictate international affairs.

Power also depends on psychological as well as objective factors. Until it is actually used, it is what people think it is.

These characteristics of power have been further complicated in the modern period. For one thing, the impact of modern power is now world-wide. The major nuclear countries are able to devastate any part of the globe from their own territories. Moreover, they have become the chief opponents of one another. At the moment when the risks of power have never been greater, foreign policy has become truly global.

These risks are especially heightened owing to the fact that offensive power is now far superior to defensive power. No defensive system in existence or being envisaged seems capable of preventing damage incomparably more devastating than any that a society has ever experienced. This has caused the distinction between precautionary and defensive foreign policy to erode. In view of the perils, foreign policy would seem to have to be precautionary. Its aim would be to keep potential enemies from acquiring a potentially disastrous offensive power. But the actual policy of the major powers has become a defensive one, designed not to prevent the accumulation of hostile capability but to retaliate against attack—when for many reasons it may already prove too late.

This situation has come about because power is disproportionate to most of the objectives in dispute. No matter what spectrum of power the major contenders may dispose of, the fear of escalation is inescapable. Thus the major nuclear powers recoil from the direct use of force against each other. They have the capacity to destroy each other. But this fact works to reduce their ability to threaten because the threat is not credible and the risks are great. The major powers are inhibited also, in varying degrees, from using force against minor countries because of the uncertain reaction of the international consensus.

The paradox of our world can be stated as follows: power has never been greater but never less useful. The margin of superiority enjoyed by the industrialized over the developing countries is vaster than in the heyday of colonialism; but these latter countries have a scope of action wider than ever before. It is not their strength that protects them but the inhibitions and rivalries of the two great nuclear powers.

Deterrent power has consequently become the most significant aspect of contemporary strategy. However, deterrence is above all a psychological problem. The assessment of risks on which it depends becomes less and less precise in the face of weapons of unprecedented novelty and destructiveness. A bluff taken seriously is more useful than a serious threat interpreted as a bluff. Strategy henceforth cannot confine itself to expertise in designing weapons systems but must involve a close understanding of the opponent's calculations.

Moreover, deterrence proves its mettle negatively, so long as things do *not* happen. Unfortunately, it is never easy to show why something has not occurred. Success may seem to have been won by the best strategic theories or by barely tolerable ones. It is also possible to maintain that the country against which defensive preparations are taken never had any intention of attacking in the first place. Thus successful deterrence can furnish arguments to sustain obsolescent theories and designs, or it can encourage neutralism. It provides little incentive for the kind of innovation, political and strategic, consistent with a rapidly changing technology.

ii

In constructing its military force, every advanced country has more technical choices than it can afford. Whether it chooses missiles with large or small warheads, whether it emphasizes nuclear or conventional power, will depend more on its strategic doctrine than on the technology available to it. But strategic doctrine must not become something theoretical or dogmatic. Its role is to define the likely dangers and how to deal with them, to project feasible goals and how to obtain them. It must furnish a mode of action for the circumstances it defines as "ordinary." Its adequacy will be tested according to whether these ordinary events do in fact occur and whether the forces developed in their anticipation are adequate to deal with the real challenges.

In the inter-war period French strategic doctrine exalted the value of the defensive and built its plans around the Maginot Line. However, the likely German attempts to overthrow the Treaty of Versailles could be prevented only by French offensive action. By the time the Maginot Line might prove useful, in other words, the Versailles settlement would already have been overturned. Thus the French strategic doctrine contributed to the paralysis of French policy.

When German armies reoccupied the Rhineland and attacked France's allies in Eastern Europe, French power remained passive, and French diplomacy stood impotent. Even when the long-awaited attack in the West finally came, it turned the flank of the French fortifications. In short, French policy in the inter-war period was hamstrung by shortsighted strategic doctrine.

By contrast, the British policy goal over two centuries was to prevent any country from dominating the European continent. Aware that continental resources were insufficient for hegemonic aspirations, Britain concentrated on maintaining a navy which could confine any aggressor to the European land mass. Britain's army, small and compact, was designed to intervene to tip the balance. In this fashion Britain was able to act as the balancer of the European equilibrium.

An excessively rigid strategic doctrine can absorb great energy in the attempt to reconcile what happens with what is expected. If it is too complicated, it can break down under the stress of decision-making. The Schlieffen Plan, Germany's military design for World War I, provided for every contingency except the psychological strain on the commander. It failed largely because the German leaders lost their nerve. In the face of Russian advances into eastern Germany—foreseen by the Schlieffen plan—they rushed reinforcements from the west, weakening their offensive power at the crucial moment. It adds to the irony of the situation that these reinforcements were in transit when the decisive battles in both the East *and* the West were being fought.

But if there is no doctrine at all and a society operates pragmatically, solving problems "on their merits" as the saying goes, every event becomes a special case. More energy is spent deciding where one is than where one is going. Each event is compartmentalized and dealt with by experts in the special difficulties it involves without an adequate understanding of its relation to other occurrences. This is the risk United States policy has been running since it undertook the stewardship of the free world.

To be effective, a strategy must fulfill several requirements. It must be able to win a domestic consensus, both among the technical and the political leadership. It must be understood by the opponents to the extent needed for effective deterrence. It must receive allied endorsement if alliances are to remain cohesive. It must be relevant to the problems in the uncommitted areas so as to discourage international anarchy. Unfortunately, the reconciliation of these various tasks is far from easy and perhaps impossible.

The nature of power has never been easy to assess; but in the nuclear age this problem is complicated by the immense destructiveness of weapons and the rapid change of technology. Though risks are enormous, power has become ever more intangible. The weapons are novel and abstract —and everything depends on them. The debate over the Nuclear Test Ban Treaty focused attention on the question of the adequacy of our warheads. But in fact other weapons systems components contain many more uncertainties. We know only by theory the estimated hardness of Minutemen silos, and relatively few missiles of each category have been proof-tested. There is little experience with salvo firing, and air defense systems must be designed without knowledge of the specifics of the offense. Each series of nuclear tests always produced a considerable number of unexpected phenomena.

Difficult as it is to be certain about the technical characteristics of weapon systems, the uses of modern arms are even more debatable. What threats, for example, can one make with solid-fuel missiles? If weapons are in an extreme state of natural readiness, how can one demonstrate the increased preparedness that historically served as a warning? It is probable that missiles can perform most of the technical functions heretofore assigned to airplanes and that the gradual phasing out of bombers therefore makes good technical sense. But have we adequately thought about the kind of diplomacy which results from a retaliatory threat depending largely on solid fuel missiles in underground silos? During the Cuban Crisis of October, 1962, we conveyed an effective warning by dispersing SAC bombers to civilian airports. What equivalent tactic can we employ when our strategic forces are composed entirely of missiles?

By questions like these the contemporary strategic debate is given a theoretical, almost metaphysical character. An ever-widening gap has appeared between the sophistication of our technical studies and the capacity of an already overworked leadership group to absorb their intricacy. Since the end of World War II, strategic studies have received increased attention. At first hesistantly but with growing intensity, both academic- and government-sponsored research organizations have fed their difficult conceptions into national policy. The theory of flexible response so much favored by the Defense Department is based on studies by the RAND Corporation and has been transplanted from California to the Pentagon.

Unfortunately, difficulties arise when very complex theories must be implemented by overtaxed decision-makers. It is unlikely that even the most conscientious President can devote as many hours to a given problem as the analyst has had years to study it. He will have to work with approximations, and his decisions will have to be made under stress. Even if he perfectly comprehends the logical symmetry of a strategic theory, he must also weigh the consequences of its failure. In other words, there is a danger that doctrines of too great a complexity could bring about the kind of psychological failure which we noted in connection with the Schlieffen Plan in 1914.

Inevitable problems of confidence and competence between the technical and political levels of domestic decision-making may make it difficult to implement a strategic doctrine. Architects of strategy need a continual awareness that their audience is not a group of colleagues of similar technical competence but of hard-pressed individuals for whom strategy can be but one of a number of concerns. Thus excessive complexity may lead to paralysis. The strategists must at every stage ask of the decision-maker: Does he understand the doctrine? Does he believe in it? Will the doctrine meet emergencies or provide an excuse for inaction? Does it instill a sense of mastery or produce a feeling of impotence? What does the decision-maker really mean when he accepts a strategy? Does he accept it with the notion, "In prescribed circumstances this is what I will do"? Or does he have the *arrière-pensée*, "If this is all I can do, I will do nothing"? A wise strategic analyst will not fail to understand that technique can never be an end in itself and that policy ultimately depends on the intangibles of motivation and purpose and will.

iii

Problems that arise within a government are even more complicated within an alliance. For in an alliance of sovereign states the uncertainties inherent in strategic analysis are compounded by the fact that sovereignty implies the unilateral right to alter one's strategic views. If an alliance contains a dominant partner this problem is accentuated. Then survival is likely to seem to depend not only on the actions of the opponent but also on the constancy of the senior partner. As a result, the weaker allies have a tendency to cling to the *status quo*, which has the advantage of familiarity and is also a guarantee of the senior partner's consistency. In post-war European-American relations, the Europeans have at times seemed more eager to extract American reassurances than to develop responsible policy of their own. Moreover, in every effort to develop autonomous political and strategic views, they have run up against perplexities of a nuclear age.

Let us examine a current case in point. In strictly technical terms it is desirable that all nuclear weapons in an alliance should be under central control. But unitary control of these weapons is in some ways incompatible with an alliance of sovereign states, for it makes the survival of all allies depend on the decision of one. The clash of the American notion of nuclear requirements with the desire of some of our partners to keep maximum control over their destiny has accounted for some of the tension in the Atlantic alliance.

Concentration of nuclear power in the hands of one country raises one set of problems; the range of modern weapons poses another. In the past, a threatened country could either resist or surrender. If it chose to resist, it had to be prepared to accept the consequence of a certain amount of physical damage and loss of life. No distant ally could be of help unless it was able to bring its strength to bear in the area of conflict. Modern weapons, however, have given rise to a new situation. What each member country wants from an alliance is the assurance that an attack on it will be considered a *casus belli*. Deterrence is achieved by adding the threat of a distant ally to its own power. But each state has no less of an incentive to minimize its jeopardy should deterrence fail. In this respect the range of modern weapons may provide unprecedented opportunities. In 1914 Belgium could not base its defense on a strategy which made Britain the primary target; but in the age of intercontinental rockets this technical possibility exists.

Thus it is not difficult to see why part of the strategic dispute within the alliance involves jockeying to determine the sector of war if deterrence fails, though this obviously cannot be made explicit. To us a conventional war confined to Europe may appear relatively tolerable; but to Europeans, deep in their memory of conventional wars, the prospect is less than inviting. To them a nuclear exchange between the major opponents may be a more attractive strategy; consequently, the threat of nuclear retaliation will seem a more effective deterrent to Europeans. Though the interests of the alliance may be ultimately indivisible, this does not guarantee the absence of dispute on how objectives should be implemented.

This problem is all the more serious because the risks of modern war are to some extent inconsistent with the traditional notion of alliances. In the past, a nation would come to the assistance of another because defeat of the ally was either considered a prelude to its own defeat or involved a relative decline in its world position. The consequences of resistance seemed preferable to the risks of inaction. With modern weapons it is not self-evident that the ultimate consequences of passivity will be worse than the immediate results of conflict. If allied strategic doctrine relies on the threat of general nuclear war, the outbreak of a war involves risks which in the past were associated with total defeat. But if an attempt is made to create a more flexible response, fuel is added to the suspicions which are always ripe in a coalition of sovereign states. Color is lent to the argument that the senior partner takes the interests of his allies less seriously than his own. This has been one of the problems confronted by the NATO alliance.

One remedial suggestion has been to place greater reliance on the process of consultation. No doubt we can and should improve formal consultative processes. But it is well to remember that even within our own government, consultation does not guarantee an identity of views. Whatever the field of consultation, a decision is finally required, and it is bound to be more difficult where sovereign states are involved. Some leaders of the British Labor Party have suggested that Britain might give up its nuclear weapons in return for a greater voice in American policy. An old and honored ally like Great Britain should, of course, always receive a respectful hearing. But what exactly does a "greater voice" entail? A veto over all our foreign policy? A veto over SAC plans? What happens when views differ or if interests do not coincide? These questions involve both a technical and a political component.

On the technical level, the effectiveness of consultation depends on the competence of the participating parties. Though in our own bureaucracy, many departments have the right to offer their views, a much smaller number carry actual weight. Since the weight given to advice is proportionate to the competence it reflects, we may well ask whether in the long run our allies could consult effectively while we possess virtually all the technical knowledge and physical control of nuclear weapons. One suspects that if the alliance is to remain politically vital, its requirements will be much broader than a technical consideration of strategy.

It is likely that the concerns expressed about the absence of joint strategic planning are the symptom and not the cause of many allied tensions. If the alliance cannot develop procedures for a common diplomacy or at least agree upon a prescribed range of divergence, it would seem contradictory to insist on unitary strategic control. It should not shock us to see countries reluctant to entrust their survival to an ally, when NATO has not even managed to develop a common trade policy toward Communist-bloc countries. Harsh disagreements over such issues as Suez, the Congo, negotiating tactics over Berlin, or the defense of

South Arabia demonstrate that differences in the alliance are neither strange nor new. At present we see the United States in the curious position of staking great prestige on the NATO Multilateral Force and a system of unitary strategic control, while matters so critical as East-West negotiations or the war in Southeast Asia are dealt with more or less unilaterally.

A re-examination of priorities seems in order. More emphasis should be given to common policies in those areas where interests coincide and less to essentially technical remedies as magic cure-alls. In this process, it may be important to ask how much centralization is in fact desirable in a system of strategy and diplomacy. Is it more vital in the long run to construct a unitary Atlantic system or one that permits some autonomy? The value of united action on many issues—particularly East-West relations— is evident. In other cases, some degree of flexibility may be desirable. If over the next decades the United States finds itself increasingly engaged in the Far East and in Latin America, our European allies may not perceive their vital interest to be at stake in these areas. Even if President de Gaulle's methods of diplomacy have been original, his views on this subject are far from unique in Europe.

Atlantic policy, if centralized, might tend to be reduced to the lowest common denominator and permit the Soviets to use our global involvements to blackmail Europe. Given the European lack of interest in some of these worldwide issues, this could strain the alliance beyond the breaking point. But, on the other hand, if Europe retains some capacity for independent action in the military and political sphere, this could reduce the temptation for Soviet adventures even if it gave us no greater support from the alliance in non-European areas. To state the proposition more positively, a structure which allowed us to coordinate a variety of approaches towards the new nations could reinvigorate Western policies, the self-confidence of our allies, and the long-term vitality of the alliance. Paradoxically, the unity of the Atlantic area can be encouraged by a structure which, in granting reasonable autonomy, reduces the desire for it.

iv

Neutrality is not a new concept, but its forms have changed in the modern period. Traditionally, states have been able to gain formal or legal recognition of their decision to remain non-belligerent in war. Often this decision has been taken *ad hoc*. Thus, despite her formal alliance with a belligerent, Italy remained neutral at the beginning of each of the world wars. Neutrality can also be a deliberate act of national policy. Some states have announced in advance that they would not join a conflict regardless of the issues of the nature of the opposing forces unless their own territory was attacked. Sweden and Switzerland have made unilateral declarations of neutrality. Or else, as in the case of Belgium, neutrality may be given international status through a formal agreement of the major powers.

Whether a neutral country will be able to maintain its position depends both on the temptation it presents to an attacker and on the assistance other countries are willing to supply. The temptations in turn reflect the advantage to be gained by violating the neutrality. Since Belgium lies athwart the invasion routes into France, she has been less fortunate in escaping war than Sweden.

Countries aspiring to neutrality can rely for their defense on their own strength or on the implied assistance that other countries may furnish. If they aspire to self-sufficiency, they are likely to develop military forces far in excess of those required by a member of an alliance system. Even taking into account the difference in resources, Sweden's military power is much greater than Norway's.

On the other hand, when a neutral, either because of insufficient resources or deliberate policy has made itself dependent on the assistance of other countries, it has in the past often combined the disadvantages of alliance policy with those of neutrality. By itself the neutral was rarely strong enough to deter aggression, while at the same time its neutrality prevented it from making joint defensive preparations with a would-be protector. Belgium's position in the two world wars illustrates this point precisely. But no matter what military policy is pursued, neutrality has in the past implied the desire to abstain from close involvement in international diplomacy.

Though these traditional patterns of neutrality still exist, they have been significantly modified by two contradictory tendencies. On the one hand, the advent of nuclear power has cast in doubt the ability of any non-nuclear country to defend itself against a nuclear opponent. In other words, the neutral is deprived of the capacity to impose military risks out of proportion to the aggressor's objective, if the latter is prepared to use nuclear weapons and if the neutral cannot count on foreign nuclear protection.

At the same time, the bi-polar nature of the international political structure makes the probability of protection far greater than it was in the past. In contemporary international affairs, a country suffers fewer disadvantages from being neutral and may even gain some international stature through the competition of the major powers for its allegiance. The nuclear age has unmistakably eroded the distinction between allies and neutrals. Though neutral, India was assured of much the same protection in the face of the Chinese attack as would have been extended in comparable circumstances to Pakistan, a member of two alliances.

This modification accounts for the emergence of a new type of neutral: countries which deliberately exploit the great-power confrontation in order not so much to enhance their territorial security but to magnify their diplomatic role. Far from standing apart in international conflicts, they actively embroil themselves by attempting to manipulate the great powers and to advance their own purposes in the process.

This type of diplomacy is demoralizing for the stability of the international system and has adverse effects on both the great powers and the uncommitted themselves. By setting up a contest which by its own ground rules can be won by neither of the two nuclear giants, the uncommitted nation of this new type tempts de-stabilizing adventures and encourages political chaos. In the long run, the new nations will find it difficult to combine neutrality with incessant intervention. To the degree that the uncommitted nations can convince the major powers that their support is consequential, they are either courted or pressured. Neutrality then becomes an invitation to be wooed.

With no apparent feeling of contradiction, the so-called uncommitted nations have felt free to practice *vis-à-vis* their own neighbors the kind of power politics which they urge the great powers to abjure. Exhortations for peace, reasonableness, and compromise seem to have no logical connection with the actions undertaken by the United Arab Republic in Yemen or Indonesia in Borneo.

Thus a new element of volatility has been added to international affairs. Though many of the neutrals have a stake in the avoidance of war, they also see advantages in perpetuating the competition of the super-powers. For they see this conflict bestowing on them an enhanced bargaining position and prospects of economic development to which they could not otherwise aspire.

In their turn, the major powers are handicapped by a paradox. Though their relative superiority over other nations has never been greater, it has also never been less relevant. The use of nuclear weapons against the uncommitted is for all practical purposes excluded. The other military forces have in the meantime become less and less suitable for the low-threshold warfare that is waged in the uncommitted areas.

A diplomacy of weakness has been the result. When the uncommitted nations threaten the West, "If I go Communist it will be worse for you than for me," this creates a pattern for blackmail. It encourages many local conflicts into which the major powers are drawn, often against their own wishes. As a corollary it means that any major country determined to upset the equilibrium can do so at little cost. The sale of obsolescent Soviet military equipment to the United Arab Republic or to Indonesia can undermine the

West's position in a way that would have been unachievable by direct Soviet action. Even leaders who are not receiving Communist military support, like Archbishop Makarios, can strain the cohesion of the Western alliance by ruthlessly pursuing narrow objectives and then calling on the United Nations to protect them against the consequences of their irresponsibility. In short, the new neutrals are protected neither by their strength nor by formal agreement but through an international consensus.

If the uncommited nations today have unprecedented scope for pursuing their self-interest, they are also subject to novel pressures. In the past, neutrality was usually the posture of very cohesive nations certain of their identity and determined to defend it. But many of the newly independent nations are still in search of an identity. Often the sole link for their peoples is the common experience of colonial rule. Domestic cohesion is only precariously assured.

Thus, while the governments of many uncommitted nations are relatively safe from the traditional military pressures that have weighed on neutrality, they are extraordinarily susceptible to domestic subversion. Those countries with a high capacity for fomenting domestic instability can achieve international influence because of it. The lack of traditional forms of power, including nuclear power, may be more than counterbalanced by the possession of guerrilla training centers; capacities for subversion will be taken very seriously by neighboring governments. Similarly, the Communist advances in Southeast Asia have depended on the exploitation of domestic instability and have been initiated by indigenous forces.

The most frequent and likely kind of war is the one for which we are least militarily, politically, and psychologically prepared. In guerrilla war, superior mobility and fire power lose their old relevance. Guerrillas need only join battle where they enjoy local superiority, but the defenders must be strong everywhere in anticipation of the unexpected. No longer is the ability to occupy territory decisive, for the real target has become the morale of the population and the system of the civil administration. If these can be undermined through protracted struggle, the insurgents will prevail no matter how many battles the defending forces have won.

Moreover, the *status quo* powers are at an inherent disadvantage in these conflicts. They must be constantly successful, but the Communist need win only once. It is easy to see why the circumstances of this kind of conflict have put the West in an unfavorable position.

What makes the situation particularly complex is that there is no purely military solution to guerrilla war. Pacification requires a government capable of enlisting the loyalty of the population. But such a government is difficult to establish because of the very nature of guerrilla war, whose chief targets are often civil administrators. Moreover, for a Western government aiding an Asian or African ally, the criteria of what constitutes stable government may prove elusive. Government can be stable by being oppressive. By contrast, a developing society inevitably creates dislocations. How to achieve both development and stability, both progress and security?

Too often, there is a tendency to fragment the problem. Some argue that the problem of guerrilla war is essentially political. Others maintain that military success must precede political institution building. But in truth the problems are inseparable. Political construction must be carried out while the guerrilla war is being fought. And in many countries it is essential if civil war is to be avoided. There is no more urgent task for analysis than the nature of stable enlightened government in developing nations.

v

It is by no accident that an academic lecture on the relationship between power and diplomacy should raise more questions than it can supply answers. Some years ago, when strategy first attracted the attention of academic analysts, the inconsistency between traditional modes of thought and the nature of modern weapons was obvious. As long as an analysis was systematic, it was likely to uncover discrepancies and weaknesses that needed correction.

Today the situation has changed drastically. National security affairs are now administered by highly sophisticated men of whom many were closely involved in the early strategic studies. The academy is no longer well placed to try to shape current policies. The outsider commands too little relevant information and runs the risk of always lagging behind events. Indeed, if he attempts to make his judgments too current, the academician may become a prisoner of the bureaucracy, and his access to information may be regulated by his usefulness in pushing current policy.

However, if the intellectual is no longer in a position to offer short-term prescriptions, he has perhaps a more important role in challenging deeply held assumptions. As a leadership group grows more sophisticated, it may become more intensely infatuated with its intellectual dexterity and lose sight of the purpose of its effort. Skill in quantitative analysis may downgrade those factors which cannot be quantified. A complex strategic theory may be so intellectually satisfying that the difficulties of its employment by human beings in moments of great tension and confusion may be overlooked. It may be tempting to treat allies as factors of a security arrangement and to forget that their ultimate contribution depends on many intangibles of political will. In the day-to-day press of events, we may lose sight of the fact that we need sound general criteria for measuring political progress in the developing countries.

In all these areas the academician can be useful if he defines his role modestly. He must not pretend that he has panaceas which the short-sighted men in office have failed to discover, for the easy solutions have all been found. Our remaining problems are obdurate because they are complex. The intellectual can forewarn against the fragmentation of policy by calling attention to the inner relationship of events. He can supply perspective to government leaders who are overwhelmed by day-to-day details and are unable to give their full attention to the deeper pattern. Above all, he can insist constantly that no answer will be better than the question which invites it. In a time which is obsessed with answers, this alone would justify the existence of an institution such as the School of Advanced International Studies.

III

The Planning
of Foreign Policy

W. W. Rostow

i

As A teacher I have never been able to become much interested in discussions of method. I have the same inhibition
as a working bureaucrat. The test of a planner in the State
Department, like the test of a teacher, lies in results
achieved rather than in abstract notions of method and
procedure.

This view has a special relevance in the job I now have
the privilege of holding. Each of my predecessors—George
Kennan, Paul Nitze, Robert Bowie, Gerard Smith and
George McGhee, as well as myself—has done the job not
merely according to his own inclinations but also as the
instrument of an administration whose working style was
set, of course, by the President and his secretary of state.
The work of the Policy Planning Council in the years 1961-
64 has, therefore, been shaped by Secretary Rusk who, in
turn, has served Presidents Kennedy and Johnson, whose

41

styles and method suffused our work, as they have every other unit in the Executive Branch.

The manner in which we have worked in the Planning Council over this period bypasses the usual debate about the Planning Council. The conventional debate centers on whether the Planning Council should concern itself with long-term issues or current operations: whether its members should think or act. I do not believe that distinction gets at the heart of the problem or identifies what planning is about.

The planner does not face a choice between long-run and short-run interests: he must combine them. I have always felt that Keynes was quite wrong in his statement extolling the short-run with the observation that "in the long-run we will all be dead." In foreign policy, as in economics, the long-run consists of the accumulation of what we do in the short-run. The great forces which shape the long-run course of diplomatic events are embedded in particular decisions addressed to immediate, short-run circumstances, just as, in economics, long-run factors affecting technology, the level of industrial capacity, etc., are embedded in day-to-day investment decisions. The critical question is whether a particular decision, taken at any moment of time, does or does not move one towards the long-run goal that is sought.

It is, of course, basic that a planner should consider and speculate about the long-run forces at work on the world scene and about long-run U.S. objectives and specific goals. But a planner who wishes to bring about a certain result at some future period of time must concern himself not merely with goals but also with how to get from here to there. This means he must understand fully the operational environment in which a new concept must take hold if it is to be successful.

This social science prejudice was reinforced by wartime experience in the planning of air operations in the European theater. There the job was not merely to help conceive of how precision bombers should be most effectively used, although the building of a doctrine was part of the job; the task was, in the light of that doctrine, to help fashion a bombing program which would be viable under quite specific conditions of European weather, enemy opposition, and changing capabilities on both sides. Without highly disciplined attention to the unfolding operational setting, the most rational of doctrines would have been quite useless.

It may seem odd to relate foreign policy planning to military planning in the midst of an active war. Blessedly, the nation is not at war; but there is a sense in which the Department of State is at war. We are engaged in vital activities on many active fronts. The task is not, therefore, to make the equivalent of contingency plans for certain abstract future circumstances; the task is to conceive of specific objectives in particular theaters of activity and to determine how to move forward towards those objectives under rapidly changing operational circumstances.

As in active warfare, it is important in foreign policy to have lucid long-run objectives, defined with sufficient precision to serve as touchstones for operational decisions. One needs a doctrine in foreign policy as in war. Winston Churchill once said, "Those who are possessed of a definite body of doctrine and of deeply rooted convictions upon it will be in a much better position to deal with the shifts and surprises of daily affairs than those who are merely taking short views, and indulging their natural impulses as they are evoked by what they read from day to day." But doctrine is not enough. One must work constantly, as I say, on how to get from here to there.

Thus foreign policy planning, as we define it, is the art of thinking in ways that lead you to begin to do something now which will make the nation's position on the world scene better in the future.

There is a second definition of planning which I respect. In a sense this definition reflects the other side of my job which is that of counselor in the State Department. I quote from Eugene Black's book on *The Diplomacy of Economic Development:*

> Between the idealists, who are more interested in imposing solutions than in illuminating choices, and the cynics, who distrust planning in all its interpretations, lies, I think, a rational definition of the concept which should be nourished. Planning, simply defined, should be the place where the political leader is faced with an awareness of the consequences of his decisions before he makes them instead of afterwards. Taking the definition one step further, it should be the means by which the lines of communication are kept open between those who make decisions, those who illuminate them, and those who carry them out. Whatever form planning takes, if it does not keep these lines of communication open, there will be a mess.

There is no doubt that part of the legitimate mission of the Policy Planning Council is to contribute to this process of illumination and triangular communication. In a highly fragmented and specialized government, the Policy Planning Council, no matter how pragmatic its day-to-day efforts, remains one of the few places where there is a chance to observe and assess the nation's position along the whole front of military and foreign policy—to place what we are doing and trying to do in the long sweep of history. Moreover, this job is done in a setting where the members of the Council are each engaged on a few critical issues and do not have to bear the heavy burden of full-scale, day-to-day operations. It is the least that can be asked of us, under these privileged circumstances, that we keep clearly in the forefront of our minds the great issues and try to contribute to the flow of policy-making a sense of proportion and of direction.

Most of our errors in foreign policy have stemmed from a failure to take fully into account a factor which may not have seemed of critical importance in the immediate operational setting but which emerged as of critical importance as events unfolded. The normal and understandable tendency to concentrate on the immediate and palpable requires constant correction; and it is part of a planner's duty firmly—even boldly—to insist on the relevance of the less obvious.

ii

It follows from these biases and definitions that the work of the Policy Planning Council is concrete and quite unesoteric, and I should like to convey something of what its members do.

The chairman wears two hats. First, of course, he is responsible for planning within the Department of State and, second, he is the chairman of what is sometimes called the "planning community"; that is, those who plan over the whole broad field of national security policy.

The center of the latter effort is a meeting once a week including representatives from the agencies which sit on the National Security Council—most notably, from the White House staff, the Department of Defense, the Office of the Chairman of the Joint Chiefs of Staff, the Treasury, and the Central Intelligence Agency. Early in 1962, that group conducted a review of national security policy. The Kennedy administration had borne responsibility for a year, and it was, evidently, a good time to take stock. From that exercise the Planning Group defined a series of problems whose solution was required if the large objectives set forth by the President and his senior advisers were to be attained over the following years. These tasks—about thirty in number—embraced problems in specific regions, in the field of economic policy, and a considerable range of politico-military questions.

Once carefully defined, these tasks were assigned not to branches of the bureaucracy but to particular men. A serious planning task reflects a major unsolved national problem. A realistic solution represents a truly creative act. A creative act cannot be accomplished by a committee or a bureaucracy: it can be accomplished, with effort and luck, by a talented man who knows that "the buck has stopped" with him.

As part of his lonely responsibility he must, of course, consult and take guidance from those of his colleagues in the government who have an interest in the problem, who bear some responsibility for it, and who ultimately have to execute his recommendations. Moreover, a planner's paper is, evidently, not national policy. It is a recommendation which must pass through a bureaucratic ordeal by fire before it becomes national policy. Nevertheless, we have tried to cultivate a spirit of personal enterprise and responsibility in the planning business; and the bone structure of national security planning has consisted, in the first instance, in a series of planning enterprises centered around individual men.

In some cases these men have been members of the Policy Planning Council, but in other cases they have been found elsewhere in the Department of State, in the Pentagon, or in other parts of the executive branch of government. Placed in a position of individual and highly personal responsibility for problems which normally transcend the interests and responsibilities of any given department, these planners help to overcome at the working level the natural tendency of bureaucratic life to fragmentation and parochialism.

Looking back, about two years later, it is interesting to see what has happened to these exercises. Some of them turned out to be dry creeks; that is, the problem was clarified but no courses of action, other than those underway, emerged. A good many of them produced results which flowed directly and promptly into the stream of national policy. Some of the most interesting exercises proved to be those where the problem was redefined as work proceeded, emerging as two or three separate and more tractable tasks. Ninety per cent of both science and policy-making consists in coming, after much travail, to pose the right questions. The planning process should, among other things, force men to turn an untractable, unsolved problem around in their hands patiently until they see it in new terms which permit action and at least partial solution.

I think it is fair to say that, by addressing ourselves to the gaps between stated large objectives and current performance, we managed to isolate a series of planning tasks which turned out to be relevant to the unfolding course of events; and that the work accomplished contributed to a flow of action which has moved the nation's performance on the world scene closer to our stated objectives than otherwise would have been the case.

One particular venture in which the Council has assumed a role of leadership is a series of "national policy papers" on individual countries. These bring together in one place a coherent view of other nations and lay out lines of action to be pursued over a substantial period of time by the various civil and military branches of the government. The objective is not merely to produce an agreed piece of paper but tightened procedures of coordination in the field and in Washington. This exercise represents one response of the Department of State to the duty of foreign policy coordination laid upon it by President Kennedy when he dismantled the Operations Coordinating Board in 1961.

As for the Policy Planning Council in its narrower role within the Department of State, we operate as follows. Each member of the Council works with a very short agenda, consisting, typically, of one or two major tasks. Under present concepts of planning he must be not merely an inventor, but he must also share in the process of innovation. This means he must work side by side with his colleagues who bear operational responsibility, seeking not merely to persuade them of the correctness of his invention but helping devise practical ways of setting it into motion.

This is hard, laborious, and protracted work. It requires a high degree of selectivity and great concentration of effort. To change the course of policy in a complex government, with global responsibilities, is a bit like turning a great ocean liner in the Hudson River: the tugboat must persist. Almost the first rule for a planner in foreign policy must be a willingness to see many interesting problems go by without his becoming involved. And, as someone has remarked, Washington is a town which exhibits an inherent tendency for all the players to rush into whatever field the fly ball has been hit. Nothing would be easier than to dissipate the national asset represented by the Policy Planning Council in excessive diffusion of effort. Let me illustrate what some of these planning tasks are like.

In December, 1961, there was understandable concern in the Department and in Berlin about the viability of West Berlin in the face of the Wall. The military and diplomatic aspects of the Berlin crisis were well in hand. What we feared was that, with the dilution of its mission to the East, the town would cease to be one in which a young man would feel it worthwhile investing his life and that youth and talent would seep away.

We in the Policy Planning Council consulted other officers in the European division of the State Department, generated some tentative notions, and then dispatched a member of the Council to Germany. There we combined our ideas with those of others (including General Clay) and set up almost immediately a close and effective working arrangement with our German colleagues. Within a relatively short time the concept had become a working program, jointly supported by the city of Berlin, the Federal Government in Bonn, and ourselves. Meanwhile, a distinguished young German economist and politician had been called from Hamburg to Berlin to head the department of Economics in the Berlin city government. He worked closely with several officers in the Department to carry out a viability program which soon had technical, economic, and cultural dimensions, including programs for cooperation with the developing nations. Once the enterprise was well under way, it fell under purely operational management. Since then, the Policy Planning Council has merely kept a friendly eye on its successful unfolding.

Not all planning exercises have as neat a beginning, middle, and end, but this example illustrates a pattern. The problem was surfaced and defined by the planners and those who bore operational responsibility. An initial concept was formulated and then tested against the setting in which it would have to come to life. Under that test a plan took operational shape, and the conditions for its success were defined and fulfilled. With the plan in effect, the planner withdrew.

In a wider field the Council has sought to contribute to the tasks of economic development in Latin America, Africa, the Middle East, and Asia. As part of a larger effort in country programming, we surveyed the state of a good many developing nations. We found a systematic distortion arising from the character of the first generation's effort at modernization; namely, a tendency to concentrate resources and effort excessively in the cities and in industries designed to serve an upper-middle-class market. In consequence the countryside was neglected, and rural folk flocked to urban slums at a greater rate than they could be absorbed in industry. We conceived of the next phase of development as requiring a strategy which would reduce the urban-rural gap by creating national markets in which improvements in agricultural productivity and marketing and expansion of industrial production would be mutually reinforcing. We outlined the kind of measures required to produce this result.[1]

The concept is now spreading about the world; but, more important, we are working with certain governments and with leaders in private enterprises, here and abroad, to bring this concept to life.

Again the task was not merely one of analysis and invention but of close attention to the operational problems that have to be solved and of collaboration with the public and private authorities who must, ultimately, bear the operational burden for moving in these new directions.

Some of the problems on which we work have an even longer period of gestation and, indeed, transcend my chairmanship of the Policy Planning Council. For example, the Planning Council, when led by Gerard Smith in 1960, helped develop and launch the concept of a sea-based NATO multilateral nuclear force as the optimum means for enlarging the role of Europe in nuclear matters without a further proliferation of national nuclear capabilities. In George McGhee's and in my time, we have been proud to

---

[1] The concept was presented in a speech I made in New Orleans in October, 1963, entitled simply "How to Make a National Market."

help carry forward this creative innovation, backstopping those who are now operationally engaged in its negotiation with interested allies.

All of these cases, and others I might cite, illustrate one generalization about foreign policy planning which is, I suspect, of universal applicability. A planner must have not simply a bureaucratic respect for the prerogatives of his operating colleagues but a true sensibility for the burdens and responsibilities they bear. The planner has the great privilege of working in the midst of the Department of State at a most interesting phase of our history, without bearing the day-to-day burden of those who face Latin American *coups* in the middle of the night, a chicken war with Europe, or whatever it happens to be that day. A planner must be prepared to fight hard for his concept but, in the end, to be quite content to see his ideas flow into the stream of action anonymously, having been merged with those of his colleagues.

A second general requirement for the planner is that he must be prepared to work, in a rather old-fashioned way, alone. The members of the Council are men who, in the hierarchy of government, might be (and often turn out to be) deputy assistant secretaries (and later assistant secretaries) of state or deputy chiefs (and later chiefs) of mission abroad. In those jobs they would be managing large staffs. In the Policy Planning Council no one works for them except their secretaries. This is a rare circumstance in a massive bureaucracy and, I believe, a source of major strength. New ideas are hard to come by amidst the operational vertigo of excessive committee meetings and telephone calls and the inescapable burdens of managing large numbers of subordinates.

iii

One of the most important developments within the Policy Planning Council in recent years has been the expansion of work done with the military and in politico-military planning in its widest sense. This development stems from a widely shared perception; namely, that the traditional sharp distinction between diplomacy and the application of military power has ended. There is hardly a diplomatic move we make in the contemporary world which does not raise the question, does the U.S. have the capability and the will to back its play? And there is no military action—from the nuclear confrontation in Cuba, October, 1962, to the guerrilla warfare in South Viet Nam—which is not profoundly touched with politics and diplomacy at every point.

There has emerged in both our military and civilian establishments in recent years a deep and unforced awareness of these inescapable interconnections. This has resulted in an intensification of contact and cooperation between the Department of State and the Pentagon quite unprecedented in our history: a cooperation more intimate, even, than during the Second World War or the Korean War.

Within the Policy Planning Council there are two military members. They are chosen by competitive selection from a group of nominees. They do not serve as liaison officers but as full-fledged working members of the Council, on temporary duty, indistinguishable from their colleagues but for the special expertise they command. Aside from the professional talent they have brought to our work, the day-to-day exchange of ideas between them and their civilian colleagues represents a permanent enrichment of the public service. Moreover, several civilian members of the Council have worked over long periods of time on projects centered in the Pentagon. We seek, in short, to contribute to that osmotic relation between the military and civilian branches of the government which our problems demand for as far ahead as any of us can peer.

iv

At its best the Policy Planning Council can contribute marginally to the nation's foreign policy two dimensions. At a time in history when events press in upon us relentlessly, pinning down much of our talent and resources in counteraction, it can provide a tactical reserve of energy and creative initiative. In a period of rapid change, when the nation is engaged in every quarter of the globe, it can help develop perspective and clarify the longer-run objectives towards which the flow of policy should move us from day to day. This is what we have been trying to do. Over the past three years there is hardly a single major issue of foreign policy or of politico-military affairs on which the Policy Planning Council has not contributed a view.

Whether the Policy Planning Council is, in fact, fulfilling its mission at any period of time is for others to judge—most notably, the secretary of state whose instrument it is and must be. But it is clear that, in the seventeen years of its existence, it has come to be an accepted part of the Washington scene and the forerunner of similar institutions in foreign offices abroad.

IV

Science and Foreign Policy

James R. Killian, Jr.

i

LET ME recognize at the outset two hazards associated with discussions of science and foreign policy. The first is the trap of exaggerating the role of science and technology in shaping public policy and of claiming for the scientist a position of undue importance in policy-making. The second hazard is the obverse of the first. It is the tendency to underestimate the influence of science, to believe that it has no useful values except those applicable to the material world, and to view the scientist as a visionary and an unfit interloper in public affairs. I would like to avoid both these pitfalls. They are but another manifestation of the two-cultures syndrome.

Sir Charles Snow, who gave a modern gloss to an old debate, performed a useful service in stressing anew the importance of building bridges of understanding between science and the literary mode.[1] He later rendered another

---

[1] Snow, C. P., *The Two Cultures and the Scientific Revolution* (Cambridge, England: Cambridge University Press, 1959).

service by dramatizing the hazard in "closed politics" of the single scientific adviser and of scientific advice not subject to checks and balances.[2] In his two-cultures argument, however, he did a disservice to science by claiming for the scientist undue prescience in non-scientific affairs and by extolling the intellectual gifts of the scientists in a way smacking of scientific chauvinism. The ensuing controversy did neither science nor the humanities any good.

David Lilienthal, who has said so many wise and courageous things, was not wholly on the mark when he recently criticized the operations analysts and others who apply mathematical techniques, methods of empirical inquiry, and model methods to the study of tactics, strategy, social systems, and foreign policy.[3] Certainly there have been examples where too much has been claimed for these methods and too great an emphasis has been placed on quantification where quantification may not be really useful. Nevertheless, we need our whole battery of intellectual tools as we seek to solve problems in the areas of defense and foreign policy, and we should reject none of them or experiments to develop new ones.

I hope that these introductory remarks will preclude any misapprehensions about my attitude toward competence groups in government, be they scientists, economists, lawyers, or other specialists. I have no sympathy with "technocracy" or any other concept of government that does not recognize that decision-making must be in the hands of accountable political leaders, practical men, responsible to

[2] Snow, C. P., *Science and Government* (Cambridge, Mass.: Harvard University Press, 1961).

[3] Lilienthal, David, *Change, Hope, and the Bomb* (Princeton, N.J.: Princeton University Press, 1963), pp. 59ff.

the people. These political leaders must in the end rely on their own good sense, their own insights and values, but increasingly, as our society grows more complex, they can benefit by having inputs from specialists and scholars. Depending upon the problem, the political leaders must draw upon expert counsel from all the great disciplines in the sciences, social sciences, and humanities, favoring none above the other except the one most relevant and useful for the problem at hand.

The art and science of international relations have their foundations, of course, in international law and organization, international economics, and international politics. They draw upon sociology, psychology, military science, area studies, and history. They depend, above all, on men tempered by experience and guided by wisdom. The time is now here, however, when they also need insights and talents drawn from the great disciplines of the natural sciences and technology. Even though these disciplines may not contribute to the rationale or to the major substance of international relations, in foreign policy-making we neglect them at our peril. They offer no sovereign remedies, easy panaceas, single, all-embracing solutions, or omniscient talents. But here they are, the seed beds of a revolution sweeping the world.

It was not a boasting scientist, but the Thirty-fifth President of the United States, speaking last October at the Centennial of the National Academy of Sciences, who said,

In the years since man unlocked the power stored within the atom, the world has made progress, halting but effective, toward bringing that power under human control. The challenge, in short, may be our salvation.

As we begin to master the potentialities of modern
science, we move toward a new era in which science
can fulfill its creative promise and help bring into
existence the happiest society the world has ever
known. . . . I think that never in the . . . history of
science has the time been brighter, the need been
greater, for the cooperation between those of us who
work in Government and those of you who may work
in . . . laboratories. . . .[4]

How does the diplomat, in behalf of the art and science
of diplomacy, better tap the potentialities of modern science? I address myself to this question. In doing so I speak
not as a scientist or diplomat, having been neither, but as
an observer and reporter.

ii

Recognizing that I traverse familiar territory, let me
quickly recapitulate some of the principal ways in which
science and technology are affecting relations among nations and the craft of diplomacy.

There is first the "eclipse of distance" and the nearly
instantaneous communication of events the world over. As
they shrink the world, these technological effects are making
the entire human community an "interacting whole," a
global neighborhood, wherein almost all people find them-

---

[4] Kennedy, John F., "Science and International Cooperation: an Address
by the President, October 22, 1963," *U.S. Department of State Bulletin,*
XLIX (November 18, 1963), 782.

selves involved together, their aspirations mutually stimulated and amplified, and their tragedies, triumphs, tropisms, and anxieties transmitted to all.[5]

Associated with these effects are the increasing velocity with which ideas are disseminated around the world and the swelling volume of information. Under these circumstances policy-makers must take measures to avoid becoming swamped with information, to have the means to identify what is important for decision-making, while at the same time they must be prepared, under conditions of a compressed time scale, to cope with sudden squalls and fateful crises. Given the technological potential of surprise nuclear attack, they must also be prepared to make rapid decisions of profound, if not total, consequence.

No wonder a secretary of state must occasionally see himself as a sorcerer's apprentice, engulfed by the volume of cables pouring in every day. No wonder that any officer sitting at the informational apex of a great government, contemplating, as the reports pour in, the multiplicity and simultaneity of troubles the world over, should enviously recall the days before electromagnetism was put to work—days when Thomas Jefferson, as Secretary of State, could remark that nothing had been heard from our Ambassador to Spain for over two years and that if he didn't have word from him in another year he proposed to send him a letter.[6]

The political consequences of science are augmented by its transnational character. Today we see a complex of

[5] For an eloquent exposition of "Cosmopolitanism on a Global Scale," see McNeill, William H., *The Rise of the West: A History of the Human Community* (Chicago: University of Chicago Press, 1963), pp. 726ff.

[6] Padelford, Norman J., and Lincoln, George A., *The Dynamics of International Politics* (New York: Macmillan, 1962), p. 92.

international scientific organizations that stand apart from the political relations between governments and are not restricted by the formal channels used by nations. One estimate, made in 1962, produced the extraordinary total of three hundred international organizations devoted to science and technology, of which fifty were intergovernmental.[7] The Pugwash Conferences are an impressive example of another form of international exchange.

Some of the private transnational organizations are affiliated with the International Council of Scientific Unions, the non-governmental federation through which the activities of the International Geophysical Year were planned and coordinated. The great success of this endeavor set a precedent for cooperation between nations with deep ideological differences that has had far-reaching effects. It led directly to a major diplomatic advance in peaceful cooperation between nations: under the twelve-nation Antarctica Treaty territorial claims are not pressed and that continent is reserved as a truly international laboratory for scientific work, where the participating nations have provided for a true and inspectable demilitarized zone.

The success of IGY has also given impetus to further plans to coordinate and conduct research on a terrestrial scale. Scientists from a number of countries have undertaken a coordinated oceanographic study of the Indian Ocean. This year begins the International Years of the Quiet Sun, which will include an attempt to map the earth's magnetic field and will require coordinated launchings of special satellites. In addition, there are impending international programs of scientific cooperation in the atmos-

---

[7] Unpublished OECD paper.

pheric sciences and hydrology and in biology that may become comparable in scale to the International Geophysical Year.

The United States has an impressive record of encouraging these international scientific activities. This record, in fact, goes back to 1779, when Benjamin Franklin sent the following directive to the commanders of all armed ships acting by commission from the Congress of the United States, then at war with Great Britain:

> Gentlemen, a ship was fitted out from England before the commencement of this war to make discoveries in unknown seas under the conduct of that most celebrated Navigator and Discoverer, Captain Cook. This is an undertaking truly laudable in itself, because the increase of geographical knowledge facilitates the communication between distant nations and the exchange of useful products and manufactures, extends the arts, and science of other kinds is increased to the benefit of mankind in general. This, then, is to recommend to you that should the said Ship fall into your hands, you would not consider her as an enemy, nor suffer any plunder to be made of the effects contained in her, nor obstruct her immediate return to England.[8]

Next, there are the many foreign scientific programs sponsored, or participated in, by U.S. government agencies. There are our foreign assistance program (which I will discuss later), the International Atomic Energy Agency,

---

[8] Bronk, Detlev W., "Science and Humanity," in *Changing Patterns in American Civilization* (Philadelphia: University of Pennsylvania Press, 1949), p. 77.

and the Antarctic program. There are also the research and development activities abroad of U.S. agencies, such as the National Institutes of Health, the Department of Agriculture, the military services, the Atomic Energy Commission and the National Aeronautics and Space Administration, with more than $25,000,000 a year being expended for basic research abroad by foreign scientists. In addition, there are international cooperative science programs, of which IGY was so splendid a prototype. With all these programs requiring attention, the handling of scientific foreign relations has become an important component of our foreign policy.

Still another aspect of science and technology which is important to foreign service officers has to do with the many ways in which the techniques of foreign relations have been affected. Technology, as I have said, has introduced a more sensitive dynamics into international relations. It has provided new diplomatic tools, as for example, in communications and travel. It has caused great shifts in the character and locus of the world's strategic geography. Propaganda is amplified by electronics, and the leaders of one nation can appeal directly to the people of another. It has enormously influenced the formation and movement of capital.[9] It has provided new opportunities for achieving foreign policy objectives. Examples include science exchange programs with "iron-curtain" countries and the

---

[9] Stanford Research Institute, *United States Foreign Policy; Possible Nonmilitary Scientific Developments and their Potential Impact on Foreign Policy Problems of the United States, a Study Prepared at the Request of the Committee on Foreign Relations, U. S. Senate (86th Congress, 1st Session) . . . September,* 1959 (Washington: U.S. Government Printing Office, 1959), pp. 5-6.

proffer of U.S. scientific and engineering competence in helping countries solve specific problems.

The achievement of political objectives can sometimes be furthered by drawing upon the richness of U.S. technology, or by directing scientific activities toward important political goals—as, for example, world health, agricultural advances, atoms for peace, the peaceful uses of outer space, and world weather reporting and control. Thus science and technology provide a growing pool of opportunities to help the U.S. help other countries, to cultivate good will, and to enhance our prestige. All of this requires new skills and an understanding of the subtle relations between technological and political ideas. As the rivalry among nations extends to outer space, the foreign service officer faces a host of new problems, including some in Newtonian physics and cosmology. He must be concerned with such interesting concepts as "the right of innocent passage in space" or the limits of a nation's sovereignty above or outward from the land it occupies or the negotiations required as Comsat gets ready to launch the world's first non-experimental commercial satellite communications system. Perhaps he recalls with a sigh the simplicities of an old Roman dictum which might be roughly translated as "the soil one owns extends up to the heavens and below to hell." He finds himself involved in tricky problems, transcending the international, such as West Ford, the "Starfish" test, frequency allocations for satellites, or the risk of man-made contamination of the moon—and why there is a risk.

These are but a few of the reasons why science, whether apparent or unrecognized, whether welcomed or unwelcomed, is present today in the foreign offices of the world.

As William G. Carleton recently wrote in the *American Scholar*, "Never in history have war and world politics been so tightly in the grip of such stupendous and rapidly changing technological developments as they are today. Any predictions about the future must necessarily take into account the possibilities of future technological breakthroughs."[10] Foreign policy has to anticipate these changes and prepare to cope with them.

iii

I would like to report on specific examples, all post-World-War-II, which illustrate the relations of science and technology to public policy and which may suggest future ways in which scientists and engineers may be called upon for contributions to foreign policy. I start with case histories in which I have had a personal involvement or which I have been able to observe at close range and about which I can therefore speak with first-hand knowledge.

In 1954 President Eisenhower requested that the President's Science Advisory Committee, then a stand-by, "back-burner" group located in the Office of Defense Mobilization, form a task force to undertake a comprehensive review of U.S. military technology. In response, a group was recruited under the cover name, the Technological Capabilities Panel, made up of about forty people, mostly scientists and engineers but including distinguished social scientists and military officers, a group of experts who worked about

[10] Carleton, William G., "Our Post-Crisis World," *American Scholar*, 33 (Winter, 1963-64), 42.

six months full time. It was my privilege to be director of the study.

The results were presented in early 1955 to the President and to the National Security Council. This report was then, and still is and should be, a classified document, but there has been enough revealed about it to give some glimpse of its impact. It has been publicly stated by the Navy, for example, that the decision to undertake the Polaris missile program resulted from a recommendation in this report[11] —a recommendation that was but one expression of the convictions of many scientists and engineers that we should seek to create a hardened, dispersed, and invulnerable deterrent.

As significant, perhaps, as any of the recommendations in this report was its demonstration of the importance of intensive interdisciplinary studies looking toward advances in military technology. When properly staffed, such studies bring to the policy-maker objective appraisals free of department bias, fresh insights, and innovative ideas which executive staffs find it difficult to come by under the unremitting operating pressures to which they are subjected. Such studies are very much needed today to counter the slowdown we currently witness in innovations in military technology.

The Technological Capabilities Panel was by no means an isolated example of the use of scientific and technological panels and committees which have brought to the government the best engineering judgment available in the nation.

---

[11] *Polaris Chronology: History of the Fleet Ballistic Missile Weapon System Development Program* (Washington, D.C.: Special Projects Office, U.S. Department of the Navy, 1963).

It was followed, for example, by another major study, the provocative Gaither Report. In addition, there was the brilliant and decisively influential Von Neumann Committee, which did so much to shape our missile program, and a series of "summer study projects" with such unrevealing code names as Hartwell, East River, Charles, Vista, Lamplight, and others, which had an impact upon weapons development and on tactics and strategy. I need only cite continental air defense, the Distant Early Warning ("Dew") Line, the Navy Tactical Data System, or the evolving concepts for use of tactical nuclear weapons as examples of important military capabilities which were advanced by such studies. Some of them also provoked controversy when they challenged established military doctrines (which need to be challenged from time to time); all of them presented concepts or recommendations impinging directly or indirectly on foreign policy.

The work of the Technological Capabilities Panel and its cordial acceptance at top policy levels in government had an important side effect: it helped to re-establish renewed confidence between the government and the scientific community—a confidence that had been seriously damaged by the Oppenheimer case. It also paved the way for the subsequent decision by the President to appoint a science adviser to his staff. For these reasons it holds an important position in any list of the most influential events, post-World-War-II, in the history of government-science relationships.

My second example is the appointment in November, 1957, following Sputnik I, by President Eisenhower, of the nation's first special assistant to the President for science and technology, and the reconstitution of the old President's Science Advisory Committee (originally appointed by President Truman) as a committee reporting directly to the President. With the full support of the President, this special assistant was given "full access to all plans, programs and activities involving science and technology in the government." In a letter from the President outlining his duties, he was further directed to be "available as an adviser to Cabinet members and other officers of the government holding policy responsibilities," to "try to anticipate future trends and developments, particularly as they affect national security, and suggest future action in regard thereto," "to advise on scientific and technological matters at top-level policy deliberations," and to be concerned "with the interchange . . . of scientific and technological information with scientists and officials, military and nonmilitary, of our allies and to encourage science in the free world." The President authorized this special assistant to attend National Security Council meetings and to be present at those Cabinet meetings where matters were being discussed in which science was involved. For the first time in the history of the Republic, science and engineering were formally related to the President and his policy-making councils.

This advisory mechanism may well have a prominent place on the list of creative and far-seeing decisions of President Eisenhower. It is one which has been ratified and effectively used by his two successors. The office of the special assistant and the President's Science Advisory Committee were to be brilliantly strengthened and given wider scope by the second and third holders of the post, Dr. George Kistiakowsky and Dr. Jerome Wiesner.

As I have said, the Science Advisory Committee was reconstituted and given direct access to the President. In the organizational arrangements that were approved at that time, measures were taken to avoid the problem that C. P. Snow discussed in his story of the Lindemann-Tizard controversy in Great Britain. It was stipulated, for example, that the Science Advisory Committee had full freedom to select its own chairman and to go directly to the President if it disagreed with the special assistant on important matters. Actually, as matters have worked out, each of the four of the special assistants who have so far been appointed has been asked by the Science Advisory Committee to be its chairman, but I am sure that all of us who have served in this role understand fully how independent and outspoken this Committee has been and how free of domination by any one person. It is my conviction that the President should always have the benefit of a Science Advisory Committee which can be independent of the special assistant and that the Committee should zealously exercise its independence.

From the very beginning, the new President's Science Advisory Committee organized itself into panels, some standing and some *ad hoc*. These are normally chaired by a member of the Committee but include scientists and engineers from outside the ranks of the Committee. For each panel appointed, an effort was made to recruit the most expert talent in the country, wherever it might be found. This procedure precluded at that time having a closed group or club dominating the advisory mechanism.

And here may I digress for a moment to emphasize the importance of these measures to insure objective, balanced advice. The policy-maker should always be informed when the experts differ and told what the differences are. As far as practical, he should listen to the contending points of view on technical issues of great moment. It is important to recognize that the scientist, however objective, must sometimes be limited to "dusty answers" when policy-makers want certainty and that there are technical questions to which scientists of equivalent objectivity, competence, and complete integrity will respond differently.[12] When political considerations are intertwined with uncertain technical questions, it must be expected that the technical expert, being human, may have difficulty separating his technical from his political views, and the policy-maker should understand this. And it is of vital importance that the policy-maker not himself fall into the error of expecting advice to support a particular view or policy.

Despite all these safeguards, the advisory system I have been describing has not been free of defects nor will it be in the future. The advisory mechanism inevitably tends to become bureaucratized. Its role requires it to monitor, to judge, to discriminate among scientific and technological programs, and this responsibility tends to dampen the creative energies of the group and to curtail its output of creative ideas. This is why we need an occasional *ad hoc* group such as the Technological Capabilities Panel to introduce new ideas and to encourage "the organization

[12] Killian, James R., Jr., "Science and Public Policy," *Science*, 129 (January 16, 1959), p. 135.

scientist."[13] Nevertheless, I believe that any fair evaluation will indicate that the advisory system is serving the nation well. I must also emphasize my agreement with Robert Gilpin's view that "while the existence of the President's Special Assistant for Science and Technology and the Science Advisory Committee has done much to bring science into national policy making, the potential contribution of science to national welfare will be realized only when scientists are active in all Federal agencies. Furthermore, such a move would no doubt increase the confrontation of opposed scientific views on national policy."[14] Actually, progress has been made in bringing into government departments experienced science administrators. It is not enough to have science advisers; there must be full-time accountable scientists and engineers in the bureaucracy carrying daily burdens and willing to accept operating responsibility.

One of the standing panels appointed in 1957 by the special assistant for science and technology was a panel devoted to science in foreign relations. In fact the special assistant and the Science Advisory Committee promptly became heavily engaged in problems related to the support of our foreign policy objectives, both for the President and for the Department of State. One advisory committee study led to a decision by the National Security Council to request the appointment of an interdepartmental committee to study the possibilities of detecting and monitoring nuclear tests. A unanimous report presented by this com-

[13] Mendelsohn, Everett, "Science in America: The Twentieth Century," in *Paths of American Thought*, ed. Arthur M. Schlesinger, Jr., and Morton White (Boston: Houghton Mifflin, 1963), p. 438.

[14] Gilpin, Robert, *American Scientists and Nuclear Weapons Policy* (Princeton, N.J.: Princeton University Press, 1962), p. 332.

mittee to the National Security Council was one of a number of factors which contributed to a decision by the President and the Secretary of State to propose discussions with the Soviet Union on the detection of nuclear tests. Thus came about the Geneva Conference of Experts.

The President's Science Advisory Committee, as Saville R. Davis has written, brought "an alternative to the White House. It was one more effort to solve the prickly question of how to adjust science, technology, weaponry, strategy, and political policy making. The President needs the special pleading of his weapons makers and users, but he is helpless if their arguments are not tested by men of equal knowledge and standing who are not committed; otherwise there is no horse race. The President and Mr. Dulles now had a two-sided debate to help them make up their minds."[15]

After the conclusion of the Geneva Conference of Experts, I hardly need say, the road to a nuclear test ban treaty was long and rough, marked by both technical and political setbacks and by great controversy, including vehement disagreements among scientists themselves. I cannot stop here to report on this journey, and its profound effect on international affairs, but it has been examined in a searching judicial manner by Robert Gilpin in *American Scientists and Nuclear Weapons Policy*.

It fell to President Kennedy and his associates to bring the story to a happy ending in the summer of 1963—a brilliant achievement in which Dr. Wiesner played an im-

---

[15] Davis, Saville R., "Recent Policy Making in the United States Government," in *Arms Control, Disarmament, and National Security*, ed. Donald G. Brennen (New York: Braziller, 1961), p. 386.

portant role. Yet Mr. Gilpin concludes that "all but one of the major departures in American policy toward nuclear weapons were initially conceived by scientists: the Baruch Plan, the hydrogen bomb, the development of tactical nuclear weapons, the ballistic missile, and a nuclear test ban. Only the doctrine of massive retaliation originated elsewhere."[16]

In 1958, the President's Science Advisory Committee submitted to the cabinet a report on *Strengthening American Science*, the major recommendation of which called for the creation of a new Federal Council for Science and Technology, an interdepartmental body designed to bring about closer cooperation among federal agencies in planning their programs in science and technology.[17] President Eisenhower promptly issued an executive order bringing the Council into existence, and in the following years it has made headway in reducing areas of overlapping activity in foreign scientific programs on the part of many government agencies involved.

In the same year that President Truman appointed the first President's Science Advisory Committee, the State Department established for the first time an Office of the Science Adviser. This action was taken in response to the recommendations by a physicist, Lloyd W. Berkner, in his report on *Science and Foreign Relations*.[18] Dr. Berkner's study had been requested by the Under Secretary of State, James E. Webb, and before being presented to the Department, it had been reviewed and endorsed by the National

---

[16] Gilpin, *American Scientists*, p. 37.

[17] *Strengthening American Science*. A report of the President's Science Advisory Committee, 1958.

[18] *Science and Foreign Relations*. U.S. Department of State Publication 3860, General Foreign Policy Series 30 (May, 1950).

Academy of Science's Committee on International Science Policy. The Department of State had initiated the study as a result of a recommendation made by its Reorganization Task Force No. 2, which operated under certain recommendations of the Hoover Commission. In May, 1949, this Task Force included the following comment in its report:

> The Department is dealing on the one hand with foreign policy matters which have a great effect upon United States scientific policy and on the other hand with international scientific activities which have an impact on foreign policy. These matters are being handled at various points without adequate scientific evaluation. . . . We believe that the extent of the Department's responsibility for international scientific matters requires top policy consideration and the aid of professional scientific judgment, and cannot properly be determined in the course of a necessarily hurried review of the Department's organizations.[19]

In addition to recommending the establishment of a Science Office in the Department of State, the Berkner report recommended: (1) that our foreign policy with respect to science and technology be more positive and active; (2) that the Department of State should encourage and facilitate the conduct of privately sponsored programs involving international science; (3) that closer relations be established between the Department of State and U.S. science; (4) that the Department invite the National Academy of Sciences to appoint a committee of preeminent scientists as advisers in the field of science; (5) that the Department of State should establish a system of scientific attachés

---

[19] *Report of the Steering Committee of Reorganization Task Force No. 2,* U.S. State Department, May 2, 1949, p. 30.

in selected diplomatic missions abroad; and (6) that the Department should engage consultants to assist in the planning and managing of exchange and foreign aid programs.

In the main, the Berkner recommendations have been carried out, although not always to the full degree contemplated by the report. Thus the original program which involved an Office of the Science Adviser and the appointment of scientific attaches by the end of three years had been abandoned, in part because of budgetary pressures. But in the post-Sputnik period, Under Secretary Herter undertook to re-establish the program, in consultation with representatives of the President's Science Advisory Committee. A new science adviser was appointed—and this time his office was raised in the hierarchy of the Department to the staff of the Secretary—and several science attaches were again appointed. Recently, with the appointment of Dr. Ragnar Rollefson, the science adviser's post was reconstituted and again placed at a higher level in the Department. Dr. Rollefson was appointed as director of a newly established Office of International Scientific Affairs. As the magazine *Science* commented recently, "It is generally agreed that the atmosphere has never been better for drawing science and diplomacy together."[20]

iv

Let me now turn from these historical notes on the evolution of science advisory procedures in our government to

---

[20] *Science,* 138 (October 12, 1962), 122.

the contributions scientists and engineers are making to our development assistance program.

Speaking both through the President's Science Advisory Committee and through other channels, scientists and engineers have pointed the way to the importance of organized research and evaluation in making development assistance more effective. In 1958, Mr. James Smith, then head of the International Cooperation Administration, discussed with me and other representatives of the President's Science Advisory Committee better ways of mobilizing scientific resources for undeveloped countries. As a result, the National Academy of Sciences was requested to sponsor a study group under the able direction of Dr. George Harrar, Secretary Rusk's successor as President of the Rockefeller Foundation. The report of this group, entitled *Recommendations for Strengthening Science and Technology in Selected Areas of Africa South of the Sahara*, demonstrated how thorough research and study could improve the planning phases of assistance programs.[21]

In 1961 the Development Assistance Panel of the President's Science Advisory Committee, under the chairmanship of Dr. Walsh McDermott, completed a report, *Research and Development in the New Development Assistance Program*, which stands today as the classic statement of the use of research as an essential foundation for development

---

[21] National Academy of Sciences/National Research Council, *Recommendations for Strengthening Science and Technology in Selected Areas of Africa South of the Sahara*. A report prepared for the International Cooperation Administration, July 1, 1959.

assistance.[22] Out of these and other studies has come the creation of a research unit in the Agency for International Development. This is an encouraging move, but so far it has been possible to make only a modest start on a solid research program.

As we recognize the value of more thorough research and study in the preliminary planning phases of our assistance programs, we are also finding ways to mobilize science and engineering talent in the United States to help other nations. Let me cite some examples.

In 1961, the President of Pakistan, who had been primed by his science adviser, described to President Kennedy the problem of waterlogging and salinity that was progressively reducing the fertility of vast acreages of irrigated farm land in Pakistan. President Kennedy promptly asked his Special Assistant, Dr. Wiesner, to see what we might do in helping to find a solution to this problem. Dr. Wiesner enlisted the services of Dr. Roger Revelle, then Science Adviser to the Secretary of the Interior and now University Dean for Research of the University of California, who headed a panel of twenty U.S. specialists to study the problem.

A technical solution to this problem was indeed found, but the panel concluded that the outlay that would be required would be of doubtful economic and social value to

[22] *Research and Development in the New Development Assistance Program.* A report of the Development Assistance Panel, President's Science Advisory Committee, prepared for the Department of State, May 24, 1961. Published in *The International Development and Security Act, Hearings before the Committee on Foreign Affairs, House of Representatives (87th Congress, 1st Session), on H.R. 7372 . . . June 26-July 6, 1961, Part III* (Washington: U. S. Government Printing Office, 1961), pp. 971-82.

the country unless it were also accompanied by the introduction of modern farming techniques, such as greater use of fertilizers and pesticides, row planting and better leveling for irrigation, use of better seeds, and so on, in order to raise the productive yields of the farms to the point where they might begin to be able to support and feed the country's fast-growing population. And the panel's report to the President of Pakistan laid out specific guide lines for accomplishing this through agricultural experimentation and education and pointed the way toward eventual need for textile, farm machinery and food-processing plants, for transportation and marketing facilities—all of which would contribute to a prosperous agricultural and industrial economy. Abdus Salam, Chief Scientific Adviser to the President of Pakistan, has said, "The implementation of these recommendations with an investment of nearly one billion dollars will change the entire outlook of our agricultural economy, increasing production two to three hundred per cent in twenty years. The nation is currently gearing up for this."[23]

The second example is in the field of education. In 1960 a conference was convened in Rehovoth, Israel, to examine "the capacity and duty of the modern scientific movement to enrich the life of newly emerging communities."[24] This conference pointed up forcefully the opportunity in science education. The late Reverend Solomon B. Caulker of Sierra Leone presented the educational challenge most

---

[23] Salam, Abdus, "Pakistan: The Case for Technological Development," *Bulletin of the Atomic Scientists,* 20 (March, 1964), 4-5.

[24] Gruber, Ruth (ed.), *Science and the New Names: Proceedings of the International Conference on Science in the Advancement of New States at Rehovoth, Israel* (New York: Basic Books, 1961), p. xi.

vividly when he asked scientists attending the Rehovoth Conference "not [for] prestige projects but the answers to our own witch doctors."[25]

Dr. Jerrold Zacharias of M.I.T., the initiator of the Physical Science Study Committee that has so successfully sparked a revolution in the teaching of science in this country, came away from this conference inspired to adapt similar methods and approaches to the enormous problems of education in Africa. He organized a six-week summer-study conference at M.I.T. in 1961 with over fifty African, British, and American educators assembled to explore this possibility, with the result that a program has been launched to develop courses in mathematics, science, languages, and social studies suitable for elementary and secondary school instruction in the ten English-speaking African countries south of the Sahara. The program, sponsored by the Agency for International Development, was begun with the development of new teaching materials in mathematics during two summer workshop sessions held in Entebbe in 1962 and 1963, and classroom experimentation with these materials is already under way. It is hoped that similar new materials for elementary science and English-language instruction may soon be available for experimental use in African schools. The program in the social studies had to begin at a far earlier stage, with curriculum reform in these subjects in the United States, before attempts could be made to adapt them for African use. However, this is now sufficiently far along that a few African educators have been brought into the workshop phases of this program.

---

[25] As quoted in Haskins, C. P., "Technology, Science and American Foreign Policy," *Foreign Affairs*, 40 (January, 1962), p. 238.

This is but one of many AID educational programs now under way. Several of our Midwestern state universities have been drawn upon for faculty to help establish agricultural colleges and experimental stations in countries that have large agrarian populations, countries that know they must try to raise their agricultural productivity substantially. Others have been called upon to assist in the training of teachers and technicians. A consortium of American universities and engineering schools is currently helping the government of India to develop stronger institutes of technology, and another consortium is addressing itself to a similar task in Afghanistan.

A full listing of the opportunities to put science and technology to work for the benefit for our less-fortunate neighbors could be almost endless, but I submit again that they represent some of the most important challenges of our time, and the way in which we respond is crucial to our own future security and stature in the world community. One needs only to review the proceedings of the 1963 United Nations Conference on the Application of Science and Technology for the Benefit of the Less Developed Areas to get a view of the array of opportunities to help.

v

I come next to note some important work in the social sciences—the "inexact sciences"—which relates to the handling of foreign policy. The social sciences are steadily gaining in power and scope, and we are currently witnessing impressive progress in the behavioral and the "policy" sciences, especially in the development and application of more rigorous techniques for the observation and analysis of the factors and forces that influence societies. Increasingly, social scientists are experimenting with the usefulness of these techniques in studying international relations and foreign development.

Most important is the growing use of a multidisciplinary approach to these problems in our universities, as represented in the research programs of such institutions as the Center of International Studies at Princeton, the Russian Research Center and the Center for International Affairs at Harvard, the Center for International Studies at M.I.T., and the Johns Hopkins School of Advanced International Studies. These institutions are stimulating a cross-flow of ideas and opening new avenues of experimentation, synthesis, and understanding.

There is much experimentation and innovation taking place in the social sciences. With very broad brush strokes, let me indicate some of these approaches. Efforts are being made to identify and delineate national styles as a useful tool in recognizing and predicting the actions of nations. As W. W. Rostow has written, "A national style can . . . be related directly to the way a nation performs in concrete situations, without fully separating out the mysterious webs of human motive, of paradox, and of process which lie beyond."[26]

Extensive and carefully constructed interviewing of elite or peer groups that mold opinion and provide or influence

---

[26] Rostow, W. W., *The Making of Modern America, 1776-1940: an Essay on Three Themes.* Center for International Studies, M.I.T., Working Paper, p. I-1.

leadership in different countries is yielding a better understanding of how these groups receive information and what use they make of it in forming their attitudes on domestic and foreign issues. The M.I.T. Center for International Studies has a long-range research program devoted to ways in which ideas are communicated, especially in international life.

Studies are being undertaken with game theory and game techniques. Real or hypothetical crisis situations are acted upon by participants assigned decision-making roles with different sets of ground rules to consider. Experiments of this nature are useful for examining the decision-making process itself, but they are also particularly useful for exploring the possible consequences of introducing a new situation, such as disarmament, into the existing international political scene.

Experience is being gained in constructing theoretical models of dynamic situations in which the principal variables can be manipulated to illuminate some of the probable courses of events that might accrue from taking different courses of action. Some of these models are beginning to be structured mathematically for computer simulation. One such simulation study recently completed showed the effects of varying patterns of investment and consumer behavior, rates of population growth, and methods of controlling inflation on the evolution of an economy in an early stage of development.[27]

---

[27] Holland, Edward P., and Gillespie, R. W., *Experiments on a Simulated Underdeveloped Economy: Development Plans and Balance-of-Payments Policies* (Cambridge, Mass.: M.I.T. Press, 1963).

A few research scholars are beginning to attempt to postulate comprehensive general theories of international relations, as, for example, equilibrium theories, in the hope of generating experiments and of undertaking systems and process analysis designed to test their hypotheses. Thus such scholars begin to advance knowledge of the human world in much the same way as knowledge of the physical world has been gained. Quincy Wright, who among others has proposed a general field theory, points out that such comprehensive pictures "have guided thought [and particular scientific advances] in all cultures and at all periods of history."[28] Professor Wright concludes that for the scientist, the world of man "may best be conceived as a field, a dynamic complex of relations among groups and individuals developing knowledge of which may increase the capacity of man to know his interests and his conditions, and to control his destiny by continually recreating his world in the image best synthesizing the progress and stability of these systems of action as they change under his touch."[29]

We require sophisticated use of these new tools. Like other technological developments that are of great benefit to mankind, computers, for example, can be misused. The late Professor Norbert Wiener, who contributed so much to the conceptualization and development of cybernetics, pointed out some of the hazards. In his book on cybernetics, he illustrates the possible misuse of the computer in terms of the well-known fictional figures of magic such as appear

---

[28] Wright, Quincy, *The Study of International Relations* (New York: Appleton-Century-Crofts, 1955), p. 484.

[29] *Ibid.*, p. 567.

in "The Sorcerer's Apprentice," the fable of the monkey's paw by W. W. Jacobs, and the *Arabian Nights* genie and the bottle:

> In all these stories the point is that the agencies of magic are literal-minded; and that if we ask for a boon from them we must ask for what we really want and not for what we think we want. The new and real agencies of the learning machine are also literal-minded. If we program a machine for winning a war, we must think well what we mean by winning. . . . We cannot expect the machine to follow us in those prejudices and emotional compromises by which we enable ourselves to call destruction by the name of victory. If we ask for victory and do not know what we mean by it, we shall find the ghost [like the ghost of the lost son in the monkey's paw tale] knocking at our door. . . . There is nothing more dangerous to contemplate than World War III. It is worth considering whether part of the danger may not be intrinsic in the unguarded use of learning machines.[30]

Nevertheless, computer simulation, as my colleague, Ithiel de Sola Pool, recently said, is a breakthrough for the social sciences. "Computer simulation enables us to set aside the defeatist and partly unjustified cliché which says that the social sciences cannot predict real states of a system. . . . The computer does enable us to put together . . . a genuinely predictive model."[31]

---

[30] Wiener, Norbert, *Cybernetics, or Control and Communication in the Animal and the Machine* (Cambridge, Mass., and New York: M.I.T. Press and John Wiley & Sons, 1961), pp. 175ff.

[31] Pool, Ithiel de Sola, "Simulating Social Systems," *International Science and Technology,* Issue 27 (March, 1964), p. 70.

I must confess an impatience with those who reject beginning efforts to seek empirical methods and rational analysis which would be useful in international studies. These efforts need support and encouragement, as indeed do the social sciences generally. My reaction to those who disparage these approaches is the same as my reaction to David Lilienthal's attack on the analysts. We need sharper tools to place in the hands of the policy-makers.

Against the background of this sketchy review, I conclude with the following recommendations:

First, our foreign policy will be well served by the continued development of the State Department's Office of International Scientific Affairs. Now well placed in the hierarchy of the Department, it has an opportunity, as the President's Science Advisory Committee has done through its panel structure, to draw talent widely from the scientific community.

Second, the Department of State should recruit into its foreign service more young scientists and engineers as they finish their education. Too many now assume that no opportunity exists for them in the foreign service.

Third, there is an opportunity in our universities to offer graduate seminars in science and foreign policy, just as a few universities are now offering seminars in science and government with good success. Scholarly literature is now beginning to appear in the field of science and government, but so far there is very little dealing with science and foreign policy.

Fourth, the productive interchange which now exists between government and the centers in our universities devoted to international studies can be cultivated and enlarged with benefits to all. Especially is it important that scholars in the universities who are policy-oriented have the benefit of consultation with policy-makers. In a number of these centers there is interdisciplinary research which brings the social sciences, science, and technology into fruitful coalition.

Fifth, there is need for more research in our universities bearing on the problems of foreign aid, just as there is opportunity further to develop the research unit now established in AID.

Quite apart from specific substantive inputs which science and technology can make to foreign policy, these five measures can do much to help science serve diplomacy and make it possible for diplomacy to contribute to the strength of science and engineering.

Finally, in emphasizing what science can do for American diplomacy, one must conclude that its greatest contribution will be a high quality of achievement. Outstanding accomplishments in pure and applied science can bring our society poise, strength, and prestige.

The nation which demonstrates the power of intelligence to enhance man's understanding and thus each man's dignity, and that embraces the vision of exploiting the potential of science as a noble, intellectual adventure will appeal widely and deeply to the best hopes and aspirations of all men. Our foreign policy needs to keep this goal steadily before it.

V

Diplomacy and the New Economics

Adolf A. Berle

i

OVER TIME, DIPLOMACY has changed very little, whereas economics, on the other hand, has changed a great deal. Fundamentally, diplomacy is still a method of communication and of presenting arguments whose validity depends not merely on their intellectual validity but also on forces giving them weight beyond considerations of mere logic. These forces are political—operating inside and outside the country to which diplomatic arguments are addressed— and economic and, of course, military. All three forces are closely interlocked. Foreign offices have always sought to manipulate any and all of the three elements as support for the diplomatic moves they make to reach objectives.

The great change has been in economics. During the period between the two world wars, it evolved from a system of philosophical or economic speculation into a science, albeit one in infancy. On the scientific base, economic engineering—use of economic force to achieve intended ends—

has come to be possible, though its scope is still rudimentary. Economic forces thus are no longer phenomena of nature whose impact may be alleviated but whose dynamics are beyond control. Social and economic conditions, national or (to a lesser extent) international, have begun to be susceptible of a measure of control and therefore, to that extent, have become a matter of choice. From that development a changed diplomatic outlook results.

ii

Economic considerations are not new in modern diplomacy. One need only recall the loans made through private bankers to Czarist Russia under the influence of the French government, designed to provide a basis for the Franco-Russian alliance after France's defeat in the Franco-Prussian War of 1870. Of like character was the inter-war financing arranged by the French government for the "Little Entente" countries shortly after World War I, designed to buttress the victorious French position in Central Europe. Again, in the decade of the twenties, two loans were arranged by the United States to the Weimar Government of Germany, known to history as the "Dawes Plan" and "Young Plan" loans. Illustrations could be multiplied; but it is enough to note that for many decades—if not centuries—foreign offices have dealt with economic problems in conjunction with their diplomatic objectives, though, as a rule, they considered economic tools subordinate to political ends.

Today the emphasis has changed. The change may not be permanent, though it is likely to remain as it now is in the foreseeable future. Mid-twentieth-century conception, largely under American influence, has placed economic and social considerations in at least equal rather than second rank—that is, has tended, though not uniformly, to give them rank equal with, and frequently independent of, direct political objectives.

No better exposition can be given than the contrast between the economic considerations prevailing after World War I and those prevailing after World War II. In December, 1918, after the armistice had ended fighting in World War I, the Paris Peace Conference convened to draft a treaty of peace with Germany. One economic issue only was seriously debated. The premise was that Germany ought to pay the cost of the war. The problem was to fix and apportion the reparations figure and to devise means to collect payment, in cash or kind, at least of the earlier installments. This was the principal task of economists at that conference. The "economic clauses" of the Treaty of Versailles—they read strangely today—were almost entirely directed toward this end. In the spring of 1919, a young economics expert attached to the staff of the British delegation, by name John Maynard Keynes, created a mild flutter by resigning in protest. Returning to England (in some disgrace), he produced a book, *The Economic Consequences of the Peace*. It made both history and his own reputation.

He demonstrated with clarity, first, that collection of "reparations" on any scale like that contemplated was an economic impossibility; also, that to the extent such collections could proceed, they probably would entail ruinous losses to much of British, French, and other Allied industry, as well as to the economics of the Central Powers. Finally, he maintained that creation of a permanently depressed economic area of the size of Germany would be a permanent drag and danger to the economics of the rest of the world. Events of the inter-war era proved him right.

Inter-war economic evolution intensified Keynes' thesis. Growing population, growing international exchange, higher concentration in industry of all kinds, combined to make world economics more nearly integrated than it had been prior to World War I. The doctrine of "inter-dependence" propounded by Franklin Roosevelt in connection with the economy of the United States was no less applicable to the international community, at least in the Western world. In result, by the close of World War II problems of post-war reconstruction presented themselves in almost exactly opposite light from that prevailing at Versailles. Instead of seeking to impose economic deprivation on the conquered foe (though this was proposed, and soon rejected, in the so-called Morgenthau Plan), the real task appeared to be that of reconstituting the areas of victor and vanquished alike so that all could enter into the process of production and exchange. In over-simplified generalization, this meant recognizing that any depressed area, anywhere, was by the degree to which it was depressed a drag on the prosperity and well-being of every country in the world. National interests, as well as decent human sentiment, dictated an endeavor to bind up the wounds.

In the ensuing movement to give the concept reality, the United States took the lead position. I personally am proud of the record of my country and refuse to join the currently fashionable chorus denigrating American action. We need not, of course, be too self-righteous. We had held the lead position in the war and in the victory, and our economic organization was the strongest in the world. But we did accurately apprehend and practically approach the post-World-War-II conditions, shouldering responsibility with that large and generous conception which was the great legacy of Franklin Roosevelt to the new era.

In 1944, there met in my office in the State Department a working group drawn together for the purpose of developing plans for post-war reconstruction. My notes on a working paper developed as a result are the basis for the following paragraphs.

The premises on which we acted were these. Three armies were likely to meet somewhere in Europe but presumably in German-held territory—the American, the British, and the Soviet forces. This, presumably, would end the Western phase of World War II. Since most of Western Europe (everything west of Russia, in fact, except Spain and Sweden) had been under control of the Nazi Empire, its fall would transfer power over and responsibility for the entire area to the Allied command. The combined military forces would have control of all transport, of most of the flow of food and goods, and of most of the manufacture. The currency system would consist of circulating scrip issued by the Allied army headquarters and occupation forces.

At that moment, national boundaries would have little economic significance. Transit would follow the lines of army communication, paying little attention to geographical frontiers. Tariffs for the moment would be nonexistent. Intra-area problems of foreign exchange for a time would not arise: the occupation scrip would circulate generally throughout the newly liberated area. For one fluid moment, Western Europe would be unified and could thus carry on trade as a single economic area, free from nationalist trammels. If that unified area—or most of it—could be preserved for a period of time, some of the influences arising in Western Europe which twice in a generation had spawned war for the entire world might be reduced or perhaps eliminated.

Note was taken of the fact that all parties to the Declaration by the United Nations (in whose drafting I had taken part) were committed, at least *pro forma*, to a number of objectives stated in the Atlantic Charter, of which three should be quoted:

> Fourth, they will endeavor, with due respect for their existing obligations, to further the enjoyment by all States, great or small, victor or vanquished, of access, on equal terms, to the trade and to the raw materials of the world which are needed for their economic prosperity;
>
> Fifth, they desire to bring about the fullest collaboration between all nations in the economic field with the object of securing, for all, improved labor standards, economic advancement and social security;
>
> Sixth, after the final destruction of the Nazi tyranny, they hope to see established a peace which will afford to all nations the means of dwelling in safety within their own boundaries, and which will afford assurance that all the men in all the lands may live out their lives in freedom from fear and want.

To give effect to this policy, it was believed that "the government of the United States should . . . take the view that it desires to see Europe west of the Russian border as finally drawn, established as a cooperative continental system economically unified in certain major particulars."

As economic common denominators, certain factors seemed most necessary: inland transport, consultative arrangements regarding customs duties, consultative cooperative relationships regarding banking and currency, accord on agriculture policy, consultative—possibly cooperative—arrangements with regard to labor standards and social security. Also, a cooperative relationship in regard to a limited number of industries already highly cartelized was needed.

In consequence, several, and especially three, interallied working groups were presently evolved. One, the European Inland Transport Committee, sought to set up a plan for unified West European operation of railroad and transport communications. A second sought a like plan for coal and steel production. A third projected international monetary and credit arrangements. None was wholly successful—in the summer of 1944 the Soviet Union withdrew, heralding the beginning of what today is called the "Cold War." Yet the concept survived in certain permanent institutions, notably the European Inland Transport Organization, the Coal and Steel Community, and the Bretton Woods arrangements creating the International Monetary Fund and the World Bank. Later, through Jean Monnet's effort, tariff cooperation came into being as the European Common Market. The contrast with the economic diplomacy of 1919 could not be more marked.

iii

The change in economic theory, which I noted in my introduction, plus a state of fact and two premises have governed post-World-War-II economic diplomacy.

The state of fact was—and is—that no small nation, and perhaps even no large nation, can exist comfortably except as part of some larger economic system. Ideally such a system should be worldwide. Factually, two rival systems have existed—that of the West in which the United States is the largest factor; and that of the Communist world, in which the Soviet Union is predominant. Recently we have seen a break between the Soviet Union and the Chinese Communist regime. It would appear probable that economic as well as political arrangements between the two have been upset—some certainly have—though the exact situation is still not clear. My impression is that the Chinese are endeavoring to erect a third rival economic system and to some extent will be able to do so.

Factually, the so-called under-developed nations and small nations generally have no alternative save to join one or other of the large systems. Occasionally (and esoterically) border countries endeavor (and from time to time they may succeed) to work out trade and economic relationships with more than one of these systems (Yugoslavia and Egypt are cases in point). But it seems unlikely that such arrangements can continue indefinitely unless the great systems finally reach a measure of adjustment, as every sane man hopes they will. Obviously they will not do so while (as at present) they are politically and militarily at each other's throats, each seeking to conquer or destroy the other.

I am aware, of course, of the elaborate propaganda commonly called "nationalist," carried on in many countries for "independence." On examination it appears little more than political sloganeering. Countries which are most vociferous in asking "independence" are equally most insistent on credit assistance from and preferential entry into the markets of the greater countries in one or another of the blocs. Newly formed African states hotly demand preference for their products in the markets of the very Western European countries they violently denounce as "imperalist." Pro-Communist nationalist movements in some Latin American countries virulently attack the United States but at the same time and with equal violence insist that the United States shall arrange to buy their products at protected or artificially maintained prices. The inconsistency need not be labored. Factually, trade of any kind connotes a high degree of cooperation, and agreement on a system of law protecting the operations of contract, transport, payment, and exchange. This requires a fairly high level of political cooperation. In any accurate appreciation of modern economics, pure "independence"—for anyone, even the largest—is an illusion.

The largest countries—the United States, the Soviet Union, China—might perhaps undertake to set up economic autarchy within their own borders. For the first time, perhaps, in history, modern technique makes this almost (though not completely) possible. The United States can (though she does not) produce practically everything she needs except coffee, and chemists may even produce a viable substitute for that. With adequate territory and sufficient affluence, and very high technology, the autarchic possibility seems almost within reach. Yet, even for the greatest countries, autarchy would be expensive. For small countries, it is at present out of the question.

Politically, however, the adoption of such an objective by the great powers would necessarily mean a multiplying number of small countries in continuously greater distress, necessarily becoming enemies of their great autarchic neighbors. Desertion or exclusion, not trade, is now the true method of oppression. This would be not only immoral; it would be unsafe. Hazards would be intensified by growing population pressure. The fact-situation of modern international economics thus really eliminates the concept of true "independence" in economic life, whether we or any others like it or not.

Of the two governing premises, the first adopted by practically all the Western powers has been simply this: Their national interests are served by assisting in bringing about a high degree of development and prosperity in the countries with which they deal. Achieving this (as far as we now can see) is possible only in one of two ways. One is to take over the smaller countries outright, making them part of a new imperial system. This has not been the policy of the United States since the dawn of the twentieth century, nor is it the policy now either of France, Great Britain, Italy, Japan, or Germany. The United States made her decision more than half a century ago, when a number of countries fell to the United States by conquest after the Spanish American War. The good sense of the country rejected the imperial solution. Cuba was given independence and endowed with preferential access to the American market for sugar. The Philippine archipelago was promised independence, which it duly received. Puerto Rico invented and freely adopted a novel status, that of an associated commonwealth which she now has. It is a realistic arrangement recognizing that Puerto Rico is a tiny island sixty miles long and forty miles wide whose cultural autonomy is fiercely preserved but whose economic progress is best served by remaining within the American monetary and trade system. As President Lyndon Johnson, when speaking to the Associated Press news publishers on April 20, put it with concise accuracy, the freedom and security of the United States is best served by friendly relations with free and secure peoples around her.

Communist empires have taken a different view. Despite their cries against "imperalism," they frankly and bluntly conquered the peripheral countries—the Soviet Union taking those of the Iron Curtain in mid-Europe and later Cuba, while Communist China conquered and seized North Korea and North Viet Nam, and now seeks to conquer Laos, Cambodia, and the rest of Indo-China. In these cases trade and economic relations have been imposed from the imperial centers, Moscow or Peking. They were carried out through barter arrangements in which more often than not (as might be expected) the conquered countries, now Communist captives, got the short end of the stick. Yugoslavia left the Moscow bloc precisely because of the oppressive nature of these arrangements.

In this form of empire, as in its older forms, I believe the political balance increasingly shifts against the imperial power. Specifically, the task of retaining domination re-

quires greater economic output from the imperial country
than can be recouped by exploiting the conquered country.
The most recent Russian adventure—Cuba, begun in late
1959—has proved economically disastrous both for the
Soviet Union and for Cuba. My own opinion is that the
imperial solutions of the Communist systems will increasingly prove as unviable now as the West European imperialist solutions conceived in the nineteenth century
proved to be in the mid-twentieth.

The alternative policy—the attempt to build the smaller
countries into viable and prosperous cooperating economic
units—has been the policy fostered by the United States.
A principal tool has been and still is access to the American
market. The smaller countries involved, because they cannot be self-sufficient (an impossibility in under-developed
countries), must be in position to enter markets and find
development capital; the United States in one or another
form could and has offered both. One notes an ironic re-
versal of the Marxian formula. Observing the mid-nine-
teenth century, Marx assumed that countries would need to
force their empire on weaker nations in order to conquer
larger markets and argued that that urge made the imperialist drive inevitable. In mid-twentieth century, to the
contrary, the under-developed nations seem driven to find
markets in the larger and more highly developed countries.
Since apparently their welfare contributes to that of the
larger countries, a formula of cooperation has to be sought.

The second premise is moral (there is mixture of motive
in international as well as in personal affairs). The large
and prosperous country found it morally repugnant to live
next door to countries whose chronic state was misery. The

nineteenth century had adopted the doctrine of a famous
hymn:

> The rich man in his castle,
> The poor man at his gate,
> God made them high and low,
> And ordered their estate.

Those who did not ascribe the conditions to the will of God
nevertheless accepted it as that of Mr. Malthus. The
twentieth century, on the contrary, was highly dubious
whether God had anything to do with this, while modern
protective methods were increasingly demonstrating that
the Malthusian formula could be overcome. The United
States for one rejected the notion that this contrast between
affluence and misery made sense. So it came about, perhaps
for the first time in world economics, that the most highly
developed countries increasingly accepted and now recognize the moral duty to reduce the difference. As noted,
there was also a strong and justified belief that the misery
of under-developed countries constituted a drag on the
prosperity of other countries.

Out of the fact situation described and the two premises
here noted, a dominant branch of modern diplomacy has
emerged. It has taken many forms.

iv

The major manifestation was the successful post-war
attempt to reconstitute countries principally ravaged by the
war itself, known as the Marshall Plan. Simultaneously

came recognition that certain underlying conditions would have to be changed before approach along those lines could be successful. Largely due to the genius of a Frenchman, Jean Monnet, Europe began to escape from the narrow nationalism dominating economics prior to World War II —the nationalism the United States working group had hoped to eliminate in 1944. Under the pre-war scheme of things, each nation guarded its own interest, its own markets, its own manufacturing establishments, its own enterprise, as often as not by excluding others from those markets and by making political arrangements with other countries, securing preference for its own products and interests at its neighbors' expense.

True, there had been breaches in this narrow nationalist framework even before World War II. But these were accomplished not by governments but by private business cartel arrangements. I think of the Achnacarry Agreement for cooperation between the major oil companies in 1928. These companies, having carried on a lively trade war all over the world, finally made a peace treaty among themselves—Shell Oil Company and Standard Oil Company of New Jersey having taken the lead. Despite condemnation of these agreements by American antitrust law, my impression is that the net result was favorable to the world in general as well as to the oil companies, though they certainly did not lose by the arrangement. Objection to such arrangements, of course, was not that they were inherently evil but that they were made by private corporations nonrepresentative of public interest. It was Jean Monnet and Paul Van Zeeland who erected the theory that such arrangements could be made *within* a framework of public control and public interest and that in Europe such an arrangement would be a useful or perhaps necessary sub-structure to European cooperation under the Marshall Plan.

From the reconstruction initiative came institutional real ity: first, the European Coal and Steel Community; later, the European Common Market; and on the purely financial side, the European Payments Union and a series of credit arrangements freeing trade from momentary fluctuations of foreign exchange. How far this movement has gone is evidenced by the April, 1964, issue of the bulletin of the European Community (composed of the Common Market, the Coal and Steel Community, EURATOM, and similar organizations). Already the European Economic Coopera-tion member countries are discussing a single council of ministers for the Common Market Six; creation of a com-mon executive; strengthening of the European Parliament which sits at Strasbourg. The deadline set is January 1, 1967. Rudimentary financial machinery for the unit is proposed; meantime, a more or less united Western Euro-pean market gives instructions to its delegate to the current United Nations conference at Geneva to present the common position of a bloc of six countries—the same six which, thirty-five years ago, were at each other's throats.

In Latin America, a generation or two behind the Euro-pean development, a like movement is now going forward. One area—Central America—already has its common market and its Central American International Bank and is already discussing the possibility of a common currency or its equivalent for the five countries involved. A some-what similar movement in South America, LAFTA (Latin American Free Trade Association), is less advanced—due chiefly, I think, to geographic factors—but appears also to be making progress. In Latin America, the arrangements could succeed only if supported by the major countries involved. In the Latin American case, assistance from the United States, offered through the Alliance for Progress, has already proved useful. As cooperation increasingly undergirds the Alliance for Progress, hope grows that the vast Alliance campaign will prove successful. It is, indeed, the only possible alternative to an imperial approach—and this the United States has long since discarded.

As in the case of Europe, the attempt to cope with economic problems in Latin America has thus produced a series of international institutions. The InterAmerican Development Bank is perhaps the most conspicuous; the Alliance for Progress has produced its own international economic advisory machinery. These reflect the groping for permanent, workable, trans-national institutions in the field of finance and trade arrangements.

Regional progress has thus been considerable. Less progress has been made on a worldwide basis, though there also the same groping appears. The United Nations conference on trade and development, meeting at Geneva in April, 1964, was in essence an endeavor to find worldwide norms for tariff, trade, and maintained-price arrangements. The May conference of Gatt (nicknamed the "Kennedy Round") wrestled with the major problems of trade in agricultural products. On the worldwide basis, negotiations increasingly are between the already constituted regional blocs. The United States, by reason of her size, constitutes a bloc in itself comparable to the entire European Common Market. That grouping in turn has to deal with the so-called

"Outer Seven," including Great Britain, while Great Britain is herself at the center of those British Commonwealth countries working with her.

Out of such congeries of organizations the new international economics seeks to achieve establishment. Diplomacy now addresses itself to this series of problems, adding them to the traditional list of military, political, and territorial questions more conventionally within its scope. Let us, for a moment, pull the problem down from the ponderous and complicated machinery into the purview of simple humanity. Three years ago, I was in Africa, following an earlier trip to Central America. The price of coffee had fallen disastrously; all coffee-producing countries were seeking a stabilization agreement in which the market of the United States and the price paid by the American consumer played a major role. Guatemalan and Costa Rican finance ministers, as well as individual coffee-growers, had passionately pleaded the difficulties involved in the fluctuating price. They sought a preferred position in the American market. Later I was at the Kilema Mission, on the slope of Mount Kilimanjaro in Tanganyika. Again coffee was the subject of discussion. I observed that the United States had great responsibility towards the coffee producing countries of Central and South America. The Africans pleaded their position also. Our host, head of the Kilema Mission, said, "Please have your diplomats remember we have to eat also."

Let us clear our minds of detail for a moment and look at the great picture. Prior to World War I, twelve empires and the Monroe Doctrine area governed the world; between them, the economics of the world were substantially balanced by international trade. Its volume, compared to the present, was relatively low. Temporary imbalances could be curbed by fluctuations in foreign exchange rates and by shipments of gold. The empires centralized the banking and exchange problem. European, particularly British, finance was organized to deal with it; at the relatively low level then prevailing, the machine worked. Then came World War I and its sequel. Four empires, the Austrian, the German, the Russian, and the Turkish, broke up. The balance no longer worked. A desperate attempt to put the world back on the gold standard—achieving balance through international loans (privately made), limited reserve-bank arrangements, and shipments of gold—finally broke down. It has never been fully restored. In place of it came the now familiar combination of payment unions and clearing arrangements, pools of international credits, direct aid under some circumstances and to some countries, a degree of organization of capital movements, and price stabilization agreements (like those prevailing in sugar and now proposed for coffee), aided by various private arrangements in non-governmental business. Since these clearly were not going to be sufficient unless all of the countries involved reached a higher production or at least a higher gross national product than they had been achieving, straight development work began to take a growing position—as it now has a central position in the Latin American arrangements.

In Geneva in April, 1964, a brilliant Argentine economist, Raul Prebisch, argued at the United Nations conference on trade and development that the least developed countries will shortly, unless measures are taken, find themselves so disadvantaged as to be oppressed; and he urged "a decision to transfer in one way or another, to the countries exporting primary commodities the extra income accruing to the industrial countries as a result of the deterioration in the terms of trade." He forecast that the trade gap between the developed and the under-developed countries by 1970 would reach an order of magnitude of about twenty billion dollars.

Prebisch's diagnosis of the difficulty was quite simply this. The developed countries sell manfacturing products at a stable and more usually a rising price level. Demand for their products by under-developed countries accelerates. The least developed countries on the other hand sell primary products. These do not enjoy administered prices and are highly competitive. Their prices tend to fall. Hence built-in conflict.

The situation is not unlike that which prevailed in the United States until passage of the Agricultural Adjustment Acts in 1933. It may be recalled that farm-sector prices and income tended to fall, while manufacturing prices tended to rise. Distress in farm areas bred endemic political unrest. Eventually a principle was worked out, that of "parity"—that is, support-prices for agricultural products at a price-index level equivalent to the price-index level of manufactured products. While the result has presented problems, in this case over-production, the greatest problem, growing misery in agriculture, was largely removed. What the under-developed countries are asking now is in effect a variety of "parity," and this is the question currently under discussion by the United Nations conference on trade and development.

The United Nations conference, of course, can only recommend. But on May 4, 1964, the "Kennedy Round" Gatt negotiations began, aimed at lowering trade barriers. Agreements in Gatt do bind the governments involved. Among these governments are those which have preferential arrangements: France with her former French colonies in Africa and the United States in respect of sugar and coffee, to take only two. Plainly the deep problem and the more restricted attack on it via Gatt are likely to converge. Prebisch believes that the rising wage levels which contribute to the prosperity of the workmen of United States and of Western Europe absorb the advantages of technical development—and concomitantly mean that their products cannot be made available to the less developed countries through lower prices. Hence the deteriorating exchange position of these countries and their growing disadvantage in foreign markets.

Yesterday, these problems would have had to be met by national governments acting alone. Today they can be brought before regional groups and, through the United Nations, before the world community (to the extent that one exists). International social and economic health has become an end in itself.

v

Results of the evolution have rather strikingly changed institutional diplomacy. Given the fact situation—and the premises—purely bilateral arrangements gradually yield to conferences involving a number of nations. These in turn become institutionalized, giving rise to an international bureaucracy (the "Secretariats" of the institutions). These are generating a reserve of men steadily drawn on for the governing boards and staffs of the new institutions and as delegates to the periodic conferences which determine their policy. Necessarily these men must either be trained in economics themselves or must depend upon economic advisers. The mere function of understanding what effects will flow from any specific measures proposed is staggering in itself. It is paralleled by the greater task of securing governmental (and perhaps also popular) assent to or for the measures decided on—these indeed will be controlled by the possibility of securing such assent. Economic diplomacy—like any other form of politics—is still the art of the possible.

To these tasks must be added the work of endeavoring to assure that the policies and measures adopted will survive changes in national administrations, including those involving changes in political parties. To take an illustration: determination to take positive steps towards the development of Latin America was first made in the Franklin Roosevelt administration. It was revived by the administration of President Eisenhower at the instance of Dr. Milton Eisenhower (he described the process in his book, *The Wine Is Bitter*). New institutional organization emerged in that administration with the establishment of the InterAmerican Development Bank. That development was only halfway along when the administration changed from Republican to Democratic and President John F. Kennedy took over. Despite the change, it fell to President Kennedy's Secretary of Treasury, Douglas Dillon—himself held over from the previous administration—and to myself, an incoming Democrat, to put the first implementing appropriation through Congress, and this we did. There are many similar illustrations.

As of now, there is an over-all international economic organization with sub-branches, functioning through the United States. There are regional organizations functioning in Western Europe and in Latin America, and less developed organizations in other parts of the world—notably Southeast Asia. The Communist empires have their own.

It is not too much, I think, to say that the framework of current world economics rests upon these institutions. Were they by a stroke of lightning destroyed tonight, tomorrow's confusion would force their reconstruction, or the reconstruction at least of some equivalent organization of affairs. Airplanes leave the Dulles Airport because of the International Civil Aviation Organization. Tariffs in Europe and increasingly in Latin America are limited, determined, and more or less continuously lowered through operations of the European Common Market and by the Organization of the Outer Seven. Increasingly, the Latin American Free Trade Association (LAFTA) and the Central American Common Market perform similar service in the Western Hemisphere. On the world scene, they are governed by Gatt. Without the International Monetary Fund (worldwide) and the European Payments Organization (Western European regional), not to mention less formal arrangements among European central banks and between them and the Federal Reserve System, foreign exchange problems would be vastly more difficult than they are today.

In retrospect, the dream indulged as World War II approached its end has achieved a surprising degree of reality. Will it endure?

Nearly ten years ago, Jacques Freymond, of the Institute of Advanced International Studies at Geneva, forecast the disintegration of the two blocs then polarizing the world. The event has borne him out. The Communist bloc is divided between Moscow and Peking, and smaller fragments like Yugoslavia have split off. The Western bloc has endeavored to absorb the implications of General de Gaulle's exclusion of Britain from the Common Market, his changed relationship with NATO, and his cultivation of Communist China. It is not beyond bounds of possibility that we are entering a phase more nearly like that prevailing before World War I. Then, great and small nations made alliances and counter-alliances, shifting as interest dictated, as they sought to maintain peace through balance of power while hoping to extend their spheres of influence wherever favorable situations could be brought about.

Cold realism suggests that this condition may once more recur. Senator J. W. Fulbright in early April, 1964, made a notable speech. He suggested that Americans were indulging a myth of rigid relationships; polarizations were in fact breaking down. We should accept the fact of Communist China, and our changed relationships with the Western European bloc represented roughly by NATO, and, apparently, the fact of a Communist state in Cuba. American attitudes towards these facts should be flexible. Aside from his observation that Cuba is a nuisance rather than a menace (since it has been held as a fief by a Communist empire it is and has been a direct threat to us), I am in agreement. But I am afraid the consequences are far more dangerous than we like to recognize. If a Gaullist France makes an alliance with a Communist China, will not the threat of China cause the Soviet Union promptly to seek an alliance in Western Europe—with Italy, perhaps Germany, threatening France and her frontier as a Franco-Chinese arrangement threatens the Soviet Union in the east? To balance this must not Britain seek alliance where she can—possibly with Spain and Yugoslavia? Are we not, in fact, rapidly reverting to the diplomacy of pre-World-War-I? Then alliance confronted alliance in uneasy balance, shifting as some strategic unit could be drawn in and endangered by as trivial an instance as that of the assassination at Saravejo—or today by Cyprus. By contrast with the new situation, the older, rigid polarization may in a short time seem preferable.

Yet at this point the new economics may offer some hope. It suggests the possibility of the inviability of the old diplomacy and the emergence of a true economic and social "third force" cutting across all the diplomatic groupings. I remember, of course, the pre-World-War-I argument that European finance had reached a state of interrelation that made war impossible. That affirmation, indeed, was made to students at Harvard by a delegation from the Interparliamentary Union in 1913—and World War II broke out in August, 1914. Yet cumulated international economics and the arrangements built on it today seem vastly greater in volume and result than a half-century ago. On the brute force side, military disadvantages as well as internal political dangers in each country would result from scrapping the current system. They seem not to impede political integration of the old blocs. Yet there an odd factor appears: political disagreements somehow fail seriously to disrupt economic accords or even to impede their increasing integration. These is a silent current of feeling that politicians will quarrel but economic life made possible through continuing international economic and social institutions must none the less go on without interruption. This current of feeling assumes, because it believes, that international economic work benefits all parties—if indeed it is not essential to their existence—and in fact has done so already.

Europe gained its current prosperity from these arrangements; so also has the United States, and so, though all too slowly, are the Latin Americans. Discord does not apparently interrupt either them or the continued development of supra-national organization. While political representatives cry out for "independence" and do not conceal their dislike of the super-economic position of some powers (the United States especially), they nevertheless demand all the rights and privileges given under international accords. Small nations shriek against "neo-colonialism" but simultaneously demand grants of foreign aid loans from the World Bank, arrangements with the International Monetary Fund, and preferential tariff arrangements in common markets where they are available. The dichotomy of their demands does not worry them—partly, one imagines, because there is little realization of it and partly, perhaps, because they themselves do not take their own political outcries too seriously. Their claims of independence, or freedom of action, or separate policy-making in the political sphere invariably assume continued international economic arrangements and apparently continued intensification of them as their base.

I suggest further material is not needed to prove a singularly salient fact. Political objectives and economic objectives cannot indefinitely be divorced. Communist countries (which have not really wrestled with the problem, as evidenced by the tiny role they play in world trade) do not hesitate to put forward their political objective—a Communized world—as a primary consideration. This does not prevent them from attacking (as Suslov recently did in his anti-Chinese polemic) any attempt by the West to urge a free world as rank imperialism—but let that go. He wants closer trade relations with the West. Premier Khrushchev's message to the United Nations economic conference at Geneva directly made the usual imperialist charge (saying nothing, of course, about the profits his own country had extorted from the Iron Curtain countries), but his agents were at the time eagerly seeking credits from the United States and Western Europe.

This brings us back of necessity to our two premises. One conclusion is that the diplomacy of today, whether it be national or as it more frequently is international, on a regional or worldwide basis, must have, and indeed cannot act without, a clear-cut statement of political intent. President Johnson's observation I think stated the American objective as concisely as it well could be: "We have also learned in this century, and we have learned it at painful and bloody cost, that our own freedom depends on the freedom of others, that our own protection requires that we help protect others, and that we draw increased strength from the strength of others." And again "We must accustom ourselves to working for liberty and the community of nations as we have pursued it in our community of states."

Economic arrangements are means to that end. Economics, national or international, indeed, is not an end in itself, but a means of peace and a base upon which may be developed a more satisfying life for peoples and individuals.

The second necessity is appreciation of the areas within which economic diplomacy can work. A spectacular example at the moment is the economic dialogue between the United States and the Soviet Union. As part of this dialogue the Soviet Union asked, and we arranged for, shipments of wheat. This was right and as it should be: it maintained the dialogue. An immediate attempt was made by the Soviet government to enlarge trade relations between the United States and the Soviet Union—although at that very moment the Soviet Union was promoting armed action from Cuba against Venezuela and carying it on directly in Laos. Not only was there not an agreed political objective, but hostile armed operations were going forward. Favoring the wheat deal, I, for one, opposed enlargement until the fighting stopped, and I was totally unimpressed by Foreign Trade Commissar Smirnov's insistence that we should at this point be convinced that the Soviet Union is "peaceful." Yet as the dialogue continues we may first achieve at least temporary conditions of peace. Then, as growing areas of peace can be established, we can increasingly agree on at least a modicum of objectives; and then find it possible cautiously to enlarge our economic relations.

vi

Space does not permit enlargement on the new variety of diplomats required as this process goes forward. For while diplomacy does not seriously change, the talents needed to present certain cases and resolve certain types of argument do shift as the new problems take form. Increasingly, for example, every treasury department needs men and, indeed, is acquiring men skilled in dealing with international exchange, international finance, and the machinery of monetary plans painfully wrought in the thirty years since the Bretton Woods agreements. Increasingly, trade negotiators are needed who understand the probable effects of trade arrangements on living standards and social conditions in other countries as well as on our own markets. Increasingly, economic statesmen are needed who can understand, for example, that the stabilization of commodity prices also often establishes wage levels for peasants in Latin America and Africa. Increasingly, diplomats have to appreciate the impact and causative quality and impact on other countries of the arrangements they are asked to make. Increasingly, they must comprehend the nature of the problems these relations are expected to solve.

Diplomacy may not be new. But the approach to economic problems has almost completely changed. In almost exact opposition to the Marxian thesis, economics must be in a measure altruist if it is not to be regressive and unproductive. This is the modern diplomacy of peace!

VI

New Techniques in Diplomacy

Livingston Merchant

i

DIPLOMACY is as old as the hills. It goes back, I suppose, to the intermittent efforts of primitive tribes to find a substitute for war when one tribe coveted another's hunting ground, its soil or water. Particular techniques in its practice have been associated with civilizations and great states of the past. The Greeks conscripted their most prominent leaders to negotiate when an enemy threatened from without and exiled them when their efforts were unsatisfactory. The Romans relied more on direct action and the legions than on talk—but they resorted to diplomacy also. The so-called Florentine school of diplomacy—of which Machiavelli is generally considered the most articulate spokesman and Byzantium the historical guide—dealt exclusively in terms of power, personality, and duplicity. The French school of the eighteenth and nineteenth century is generally considered the most elegant.

117

As centers of power stabilized in the Renaissance and as manners improved, so the practice of diplomacy began to standardize its conventions. This was an elaboration of diplomatic manners and it led—as occasionally it still does—to slightly ridiculous extremes which do the profession little good in the eyes of the average man.

Take the question of precedence. Ambassadors used to be ranked one with the other according to the antiquity of their country. Sir Harold Nicholson reminds us that it was the pope who in 1504 compiled the first table of precedence. Under it, the Emperor of the Holy Roman Empire came first, the King of France second, the King of Spain third, and so on through the lesser kingdoms and principalities. The King of England in 1504 ranked seventh, just after the King of Portugal and just before the King of Sicily.

As new nations grew in strength and old ones declined in power, the pope's table of precedence fell into dispute. This was quite understandable but nevertheless lamentable, for the disputes transcended the personal relations of prideful ambassadors and not infrequently embroiled states.

One of the worst of such diplomatic incidents occurred in London in 1661 when the coach of the Spanish ambassador tried to push its way in ahead of that of the French ambassador and "a battle incurred with loss of life among the footmen and postillions." This led to the rupture of relations between Paris and Madrid and brought the two countries to the brink of war.

Even as late as 1768 at a court ball in London, the French ambassador discovered that the Russian ambassador had seated himself next to the Austrian ambassador in the front tier. A man of action and sure of his sovereign's rights—and his own as well—he forthwith climbed over the benches and inserted himself between them. Nicholson in noting the incident laconically concludes that "this led to a duel in which the Russian Ambassador was severely wounded."

The diplomatic melees and duels of the seventeenth and eighteenth centuries ended a century and a half ago, more by the good sense of the Congress of Vienna than by a healthful deflation of the pride of kings and their envoys. On the matter of precedence, for example—so troublesome and dangerous—the Congress decided with admirable simplicity that the order of rank or precedence of ambassadors at every capital was to be determined by the date on which each envoy had presented his letters of credence. Very logical; no more bloodshed.

ii

I repeat this little history of one aspect of diplomacy in a bygone age not to try to prove that manners or small things are unimportant. They can be very important indeed. I do it, rather, to show how different the world of today in which the modern diplomat lives and has his professional being is from the days when ambassadors drove to court balls with swords at their sides and surrounded by footmen, postilions, and outriders, thus dealing with the future and fortunes of nations and peoples quite literally in terms of the personal relations of one king to another.

Much has changed since then. Representative government over at least a part of the globe, for one thing. Wider literacy, for another. Then there has been the development of mass media for the transmission of news; from the village loudspeaker for the single radio in each Chinese village to the wonder of television in North America and Western Europe, bringing into nearly every home dramatic, often shocking events even as they happen.

With the experience of two world wars within a generation—the last one bringing death and untold tragedy to millions of civilians—there is general insistence in those countries where public opinion has any effective expression that diplomacy, being concerned with the security and well-being of whole populations, cannot be conducted on a personal basis. The individual ambassador in this dangerous, complex, interconnected world cannot undertake to make in his own discretion decisions of an import which he may be unable fully to understand.

This brings me to the subject of communications and the developments in that field which have both simplified and complicated the task of the diplomat today. After that I want to discuss other aspects, or techniques, of diplomacy which modern science and new elements in international relations have made the necessary tools of the professional diplomat today.

iii

Nothing has had so revolutionary an effect upon the conduct of diplomacy in the past century and a half as improvements in the art of communication. I have no need to list the developments which have taken place. The process continues, and no end to it is in sight. The statesmen at the Congress of Vienna could communicate with their capitals no more quickly than the Romans at the beginning of the Christian era. I dare say communications were not as good, for the famous roads of Roman times had no counterpart in early nineteenth-century Europe. It was not unusual for a diplomat in the remoter areas at that time to be without instructions from his home government for half a year or longer. Even in more accessible regions, delay was far from unusual. The other day I read a letter from our minister in London dated June 27, 1786, to the Secretary of State which begins, "Sir: I have just received the letter you did me the honor to write on the first day of May . . ." (fifty-seven days earlier). The minister then referred to a letter he had written on March 4 of that year and to which he had had no reply because, ". . . we hear that the vessel which carried out that despatch sprung a leak at sea, put into Lisbon and did not sail thence until late in April. . . ."

Less than two centuries ago the ambassador of France required two and a half months to travel from Paris to his post in Stockholm. Yet I think of one trip with Secretary Herter when we breakfasted in Athens, lunched in Madrid, and were at our desks in the Department by 5:30 that afternoon.

The diplomat has gained in the speed with which his reports can be transmitted and in the number of persons he can reach. He also gains in perspective. It is difficult to maintain a balanced view of the world importance of developments in the country where one is stationed. In days gone by, the diplomat had little knowledge of what was happening in other parts of the world and there was an even greater tendency for daily events around him to assume an importance out of proportion to their true value. Today he often has more information about happenings outside his own area than he can comfortably digest.

With the snail's pace of communications a century and a half ago, an ambassador of necessity had wider and more absolute authority than his modern successor. His title, "ambassador extraordinary and plenipotentiary," could be taken quite literally. I recall the story of the Louisiana Purchase early in the nineteenth century. The two United States envoys, Livingston and Monroe, had been instructed by our government to try to purchase from Napoleon the city of New Orleans and the immediately adjacent territory. They were authorized to spend a maximum of ten million dollars. To their amazement the French foreign minister suddenly offered them half the continent for fifteen million dollars. They accepted the offer on their own responsibility, although ratification of their act depended upon the Congress, which gave its assent only after considerable opposition. I often wonder where some of our Western states would be today if there had been cable connections between Paris and Washington in those days.

Nevertheless, I do not think that the improved speed of communications has in fact diminished the ability of an ambassador to influence events. It is true that distance and slow communications in days gone by offered exciting freedom of action to the bold, the enterprising, the free-wheeling ambassador of those times. In most cases, however, this same element of distance and poor communications froze an ambassador into passivity.

On the other hand, the speed of modern communications has a tendency to centralize the decision-making process in the home capital. This development is not limited to diplomatic affairs. It has also taken place, I think, in war, in commerce and industry, indeed, in most phases of modern life, and one of the dangers of this trend is that those who make the crucial decisions will be out of touch with real, local life. In large part, this tendency in the field of diplomacy has been offset by the increasing importance of the ambassador as an adviser. His power as a negotiator may have diminished, but the complexities of modern foreign relations cause his government to rely increasingly upon his analysis and judgment of a given situation. His influence is often the determining factor in the decision.

For the priceless asset of the diplomat is that he is *there*. He is *in* the foreign country, on the spot. He is offered countless ways to come to a native's knowledge and understanding of it. It is he who knows where the true levers of power lie, as no fellow citizen can possibly hope to. His work, in Bismarck's words, "consists of practical intercourse with men, of judging accurately what other people are likely to do in given circumstances, of appreciating accurately the views of others, of presenting accurately his own." And being "in practical intercourse with men" he is, as Demosthenes put it, "in control of occasions"—which in turn can influence, if not control, events. However swift modern communications, the competent diplomat, given proper latitude by his government on tactics and timing, can perform an indispensable role in the conduct of relations between governments.

iv

Another phenomenon of our time has had a tremendous impact upon the conduct of diplomacy. This is the spread of the tenets of popular democracy (to which I referred earlier). When the powers of Europe sat around the conference table at Vienna in 1815, there was not a single representative of democracy as we today understand the term. Even in Great Britain, where a limited democracy did exist, the conduct of diplomacy was subject to few of the influences which are accepted without question today. The spread of popular democratic ideas had then only just begun. For those nations, the conduct of diplomacy was a dynastic matter.

The years have passed and the divine right of kings is only a memory, overshadowed in our own time by the appearance of far harsher systems of rule, side by side with genuine democracies. The greatest objection to dynastic diplomacy was—as it is today to the diplomacy of Communist dictatorships—that a small group of self-seeking men could place in peril the well-being of an entire nation, and do it for their own ends, through secret negotiations. One recalls the Ribbentrop-Molotov Pact of 1939. On this account the idea of open diplomacy became almost an article of faith with democratic people throughout the world. Popular espousal of the concept reached its peak at the end of the First World War, when the slogan "Open

Covenants Openly Arrived At," the first of President Wilson's Fourteen Points, caught the public imagination. That principle was made a part of the Covenant of the League of Nations, which provided that the member nations would deposit with the Secretariat copies of all international agreements to which they were parties. This was also made a part of the United Nations Charter. Although this concept of open diplomacy has not proved the panacea many of its advocates had hoped, the principle retains wide acceptance in the international community.

In democratic countries open diplomacy is ensured by the submission of all major international undertakings to the legislature for approval. In some countries, such as the United States, this procedure is explicitly set forth in the Constitution. In other countries, such as Canada or Great Britain, the requirement of legislative approval has become a part of the unwritten constitution. In either case, the diplomat must be always mindful that his work is finally subject to the ratification or rejection of his countrymen.

Whatever objections may be raised to popular influence in international relations, I believe that the most dependable alliances are those which enjoy the broad support of the peoples involved. Certainly the long-range hopes of the United States for the maintenance of successful working relations with all free nations, as well as our hopes for the eventual modification of the policies of the Communist states, depend to a great extent on the understanding we can achieve with their populations.

Despite the desirability of publicity and democratic influences in the conduct of diplomacy, however, there is still a need for confidential negotiations with government representatives, for agreements which do not have to be hammered out in the neon-lighted atmosphere of public debate. Too often public negotiations have been used as a sounding board for propaganda by one of the parties rather than as an endeavor to reach genuine agreement. I well recall that the tip-off at the Berlin Foreign Ministers' Conference in 1954 that the Soviet Union was unwilling at that time to reach any agreement on German reunification or on an Austrian State Treaty was its unwillingness from the outset to negotiate in confidence. It was not looking for agreement but for a propaganda carnival.

Often, too, the agitation of popular passions or the public announcement of a position can make an international agreement virtually impossible. No government which has taken a public stand can compromise without losing prestige. Yet the modification of an original bargaining position is often necessary to the reaching of agreement. Every democracy must constantly balance the legitimate rights of its people to be informed about negotiations which may commit them to serious action, with the necessity of safeguarding the success of the negotiations. It is no simple task to determine where the balance may lie.

There can be little doubt that popular democracy has made the work of the diplomat more difficult. He must think in terms of the entire complex of political, economic, social, and cultural forces which determine the actions of nations. He must concern himself not only with government officials but also with a broad cross-section of the nation's people. His work, in democracies at least, is always subject to the scrutiny of the legislature and to publicity of a sort which at times can damage delicate negotiations.

Let me insert here one caveat on the admitted need, in
conducting diplomacy with other democracies, for dealing
with the public, as opposed to officials; and for attempting
within the limits of propriety to inform and, if possible,
persuade the public in the country to which a diplomat is
assigned of the wisdom of the policies of his own country.
The extent to which this is possible and desirable will, of
course, vary with circumstances and from country to country. But the diplomat must never forget that his primary
role is to secure agreements and a favorable reception for
the policies of his own government from the government
which is in power. Any effort to go over the heads of that
government either by folksy electioneering in the back
country or in the rice paddies or on the local Chatauqua
circuit is no formula for successful diplomacy. Equally
dangerous can be excessive association with the opposition
or rivals to the government in power. There has from time
to time crept into our diplomatic practices the appearance
of running for office in a foreign country, happily a vice
more likely to afflict a political appointee than a professional.

v

It is inescapable that the development of modern communications and the acceptance of what I have described
as popular democracy have markedly modified the traditional techniques of diplomacy. On top of these has come—
and this is really a development of only the last two
decades—the widespread appearance of multilateral diplo-

macy. The United Nations, of course, is the most striking example of the attempt to discuss, if not negotiate, with the full participation of every member of the organization, even though there may be only two or three states directly involved in the particular issue under debate. Moreover, the United Nations itself has proliferated an extraordinary number of commissions and organizations, all of them multilateral in character. I could list, I think, two pages in fine print of permanent organs or commissions—all with multiple membership—which are connected with the United Nations.

As one measure of this new burden on diplomacy, the United States government officially participated last year in over four hundred multilateral conferences. It was involved in a total of ten thousand votes!

Then, by reason of the failure of the United Nations to provide reliable security against aggression there has been the understandable development of collective security arrangements. The North Atlantic Treaty comes first to mind. There are in addition the Manila Pact, ANZUS, the Organization of American States, CENTO, and other bilateral treaties. All in all, the United States is joined with more than forty other countries in mutual security agreements.

We are, I believe, learning slowly by experience how to practice multilateral diplomacy. This we can only do if we clearly recognize its limitations as well as the advantage it provides for the education of world opinion. But to be successful multilateral diplomacy must be reinforced or in most cases preceded by intimate and confidential bilateral negotiation and exchanges of views.

Improved communications; mass media available for instruction or propaganda; increased literacy and the large-scale substitution of democratic states for absolute monarchies; multilateral organs engaged in the diplomatic dialogue between governments; alliances with the resultant need to assist weaker members with military advisory groups, arms, and money; economic aid on a programmatic basis; and the exploitation of cultural and scientific achievements to create a favorable national image—all these aspects of relations between states today comprise what is called the new diplomacy. New techniques have been developed, notably in the field of mass communications of information and of propaganda.

The traditional diplomatic tools of loans or subventions and gifts of arms have been institutionalized. The typical embassy of a great power has public affairs sections, cultural attachés, military advisory groups, scientific advisers, and economic assistance missions, in addition to the traditional political, economic, commercial, and consular sections. The number of specialists has increased and the total embassy staff multiplied. The administrative responsibilities of the ambassador have grown enormously. He must be familiar with a series of complicated programs unless he is to lose control of the instruments originally designed to support his role as the representative and spokesman for his government.

vi

It is evident that the techniques and tools of diplomacy have changed in the past quarter century. The tools have been sharpened and a few new ones added, but on the whole they are improvements on old ones rather than new inventions. It is well to remind ourselves also that the purpose or object of diplomacy has changed not at all and that the essential characteristics required of diplomats for its successful conduct likewise remain unchanged.

Diplomacy is defined by Webster as "the conducting of relations between nations, as in making agreements," which is concise and good as far as it goes. One must, however, inject the thought of purpose. This I would formulate as the advancement and defense of the vital interests of a country, utilizing every honorable means to resolve conflicts of interest by negotiation, by persuasion, and by mutual understanding.

The qualities of character and personality which a diplomat should possess are less easy to compress. Let me cite two great professionals who have attempted to set them down. The first evaluation is by de Colliere, Louis XIV's great general turned diplomatist; the second by Sir Harold Nicholson, a distinguished diplomat himself and the son of Lord Carnock, whose career in the British foreign service and Foreign Office covered the span in history from the Battle of Sedan to the Battle of Jutland.

Let us take de Colliere first—and he writes at some length.

The good diplomatist must have an observant mind, a gift of application which rejects being diverted by pleasures or frivolous amusements, a sound judgment which takes the measure of things as they are, and which goes straight to the goal by the shortest and most natural paths without wandering into meaningless refinements and subtleties.

The good negotiator must have the gift of penetration such as will enable him to discern the thoughts of men and to deduce from the least movement of their features which passions are stirring within.

The diplomatist must be quick, resourceful, a good listener, courteous and agreeable. He should not seek to gain a reputation as a wit, nor should he be so disputatious as to divulge secret information in order to clinch an argument. Above all the good negotiator must possess enough self-control to resist the longing to speak before he has thought out what he intends to say. He must not fall into the mistake of supposing that an air of mystery, in which secrets are made out of nothing and the merest trifle exalted into an affair of State, is anything but the symptom of a small mind. He should pay attention to women, but never lose his heart. He must be able to simulate dignity even if he does not possess it, but he must at the same time avoid all tasteless display. Courage also is an essential quality, since no timid man can hope to bring a confidential negotiation to success. The negotiator must possess the patience of a watchmaker and be devoid of personal prejudices. He must have a calm nature, be able to suffer fools gladly, and should not be given to drink, gambling, women, irritability, or any other wayward humours and fantasies. The negotiator moreover should study history and memoirs, be acquainted with foreign institutions and habits, and be able to tell where, in any foreign country, the real sovereignty lies. Everyone who enters the profession of diplomacy should know the German, Italian and Spanish languages as well as the Latin, ignorance of which would be a disgrace and shame to any public man, since it is the common language of all Christian nations.

He should also have some knowledge of literature, science, mathematics, and law. Finally he should entertain handsomely. A good cook is often an excellent conciliator.

Nicholson, who expresses himself with greater brevity, says in one of his several superb books on the theory and practice of diplomacy, "These then are my qualities of my ideal diplomatist. Truth, accuracy, calm, patience, good temper, modesty, and loyalty. These are also the qualities of good diplomacy. 'But,' the reader may object, 'you have forgotten intelligence, knowledge, discernment, prudence, hospitality, charm, industry, courage and even tact.' I have not forgotten them. I have taken them for granted."

One admires the compression of Nicholson and any over-excited ex-diplomat might add to the rhapsodic list *ad infinitum*. I cannot refrain, however, from adding three more important qualifications. The first, a wife of charm, warmth, discretion, and intelligence; the second, administrative or executive talent; and, the last, a physique of at least moderate robustness.

There was a modicum of warrant in the remark of Ambassador Charles Dawes to the effect that "diplomacy is hell on the feet"—a remark which drew from old pro Ambassador Fletcher the acid comment that "it all depends on whether one uses one's feet or one's head."

Having attempted to set out the purpose of diplomacy and the personal talents that, ideally at least, it calls for, let me conclude with a glance at the state of American diplomacy. On the whole, I think our diplomacy serves the Republic well. We *do* consistently—and I think effectively —advance and defend our national interests. We have learned that, for all our power and our responsibilities, there are events and developments and factual results which occur in what Mr. Acheson has called "the vast external realm" that we cannot control or even greatly influence, much as we might like to do so. We do in our diplomacy, I believe, understand the fundamental role of power in relations between states, and yet we keep the necessary faith that in the long, long run ideas shape the world. We do have Jefferson's "decent respect for the opinion of mankind." But we must never forget that it is on sheer power— governed with wisdom and restraint—that the continuance of our civilization now depends, for "in the long-run we will all be dead."

We are criticized from time to time at home and abroad for seeking in our policies and in our diplomacy to dispense charity around the world with a lavish hand, either to do good for its own sake or to win first prize in some international popularity contest, presumably conducted along the lines of a beauty contest. The charge is unfair. To my observation, our foreign policy and our diplomacy have not been significantly influenced by either motive. A missionary element has entered into our foreign aid programs over the years. I do not object, to the extent it is in fields in which our own churches and charitable foundations cannot carry out their great work and to the extent that it is separated from what can be defined as economic and military assistance which must be provided in our own enlightened self-interest. That is why I personally favor the

Peace Corps, with its autonomous existence as a separate agency. There may well be other programs now in existence which more properly and with a reduction in public confusion could be transferred from the aid agency to the Peace Corps.

On the question of popularity, we all understand the desire to be loved. I think, however, that in this generation we have learned, and now accept the fact, that great powers with great responsibilities are rarely loved. Respected we are, I hope, and trusted I also hope, but not loved.

Let me cite in support the judgment of Sir William Hayter, a British diplomat of distinction, not long ago the British ambassador to Moscow and now Warden of New College at Oxford. In his *The Diplomacy of the Great Powers*, he discusses the diplomacy of Britain, France, the Soviet Union, and the United States. Of our diplomacy he concludes, "For all its handicaps it is forthright, generous, intelligent and powerful; it could be even more effective if it were more untrammelled."

The handicaps and trammels to which Hayter refers are in part, I suppose, imposed by our form of government and in part by the traditional American affinity for open covenants openly arrived at. I for one would not want to change our Constitution, and I doubt that, even if we wanted to, we could do much about our Yankee predilection for horse trades conducted in the open. On that note, let me end with a quotation from Demosthenes, for the discovery of which I am indebted to Sir Harold Nicholson.

"Ambassadors," said Demosthenes,

have no battleships at their disposal, or heavy infantry, or fortresses; their weapons are words and opportunities. In important transactions opportunities are fleeting; once they are missed they cannot be recovered. It is a greater offence to deprive a democracy of an opportunity than it would be thus to deprive an oligarchy or an autocracy. Under their systems, action can be taken instantly and on the word of command; but with us, first the Council has to be notified and adopt a provisional resolution, and even then only when the heralds and the Ambassadors have sent in a note in writing. Then the Council has to convene the Assembly, but then only on a statutory date. Then the debater has to prove his case in face of an ignorant and often corrupt opposition; and even when this endless procedure has been completed, and a decision has been come to, even more time is wasted before the necessary financial resolution can be passed. Thus an ambassador who, in a constitution such as ours, acts in a dilatory manner and causes us to miss our opportunities, is not missing opportunities only, but robbing us of the control of events. . . .

That indictment—more than two thousand years old—has a contemporary ring today. Democratic institutions *do* "trammel" diplomacy. I for one gladly accept that handicap in return for the great strength which our form of government has demonstrated time and time again. Demosthenes does, however, usefully remind the diplomats of modern democracies that the price of liberty is eternal vigilance and that their personal responsibility is great.

THE DIMENSIONS OF DIPLOMACY
EDITED BY E. A. J. JOHNSON

designer:	Edward D. King
typesetter:	Baltimore Type
typefaces:	Bodoni Book, Glamour
printer:	Universal Lithographers
paper:	Glatfelter Offset Blue-White
binder:	Moore & Co.
cover material:	Columbia Riverside Vellum